NORMAN CLYDE

NORMAN CLYDE

Legendary Mountaineer of California's Sierra Nevada

Robert C. Pavlik

Foreword by Steve Roper

Heyday Books, Berkeley, California

Yosemite Association, Yosemite National Park, California

Library of Congress Cataloging-in-Publication Data
Pavlik, Robert C.
  Norman Clyde : legendary mountaineer of California's Sierra Nevada / Robert C. Pavlik.
    p. cm.
  Includes bibliographical references.
  ISBN 978-1-59714-110-9 (pbk. : alk. paper)
  1. Clyde, Norman, 1885-1972. 2. Mountaineers—California—Biography. 3. Mountaineering—Sierra Nevada (Calif. and Nev.) I. Title.
  GV199.92.C59P38 2008
  796.522092—dc22
  [B]
                              2008017672

Cover Photo: Norman Clyde demonstrating, in dramatic fashion, a dulfersitz, a method of rappelling without the use of hardware. Courtesy of Jules and Shirley Eichorn.

Back Cover Photo: Norman Clyde with the tools of his trade: campaign hat, ice axe, rope, and rucksack. Note his sunburned hands, the result of extended exposure to the elements at high elevation. Photo by Cedric Wright and courtesy of The Bancroft Library, University of California, Berkeley; California Faces: Clyde, Norman, 1885–1972, :2.

green press INITIATIVE

Book Design by Rebecca LeGates
Printing and Binding by Thomson-Shore, Dexter, MI

Heyday Books is committed to preserving ancient forests and natural resources. We elected to print this title on 30% post consumer recycled paper, processed chlorine free. As a result, for this printing, we have saved:

  8 Trees (40' tall and 6-8" diameter)
  2,738 Gallons of Wastewater
  5 million BTU's of Total Energy
  352 Pounds of Solid Waste
  660 Pounds of Greenhouse Gases

Heyday Books made this paper choice because our printer, Thomson-Shore, Inc., is a member of Green Press Initiative, a nonprofit program dedicated to supporting authors, publishers, and suppliers in their efforts to reduce their use of fiber obtained from endangered forests.

For more information, visit www.greenpressinitiative.org

Environmental impact estimates were made using the Environmental Defense Paper Calculator. For more information visit: www.papercalculator.org.

This book is the result of a collaboration between the Yosemite Association and Heyday Books. You can find information about the Yosemite Association at www.yosemite.org, or write to P.O. Box 545, Yosemite National Park, CA 95389, or call (209) 379-2646. Orders, inquiries, and correspondence should be addressed to:

Heyday Books
P.O. Box 9145, Berkeley, CA 94709
(510) 549-3564, Fax (510) 549-1889
www.heydaybooks.com

10 9 8 7 6 5 4 3 2 1

CONTENTS

Foreword
by Steve Roper

Years fly by. Decades come and go but mostly go. Our collective memories of former peers and heroes thus get more and more lost with each new generation. Thankfully, biographies exist to keep certain people "alive." Norman Clyde is perhaps not well known to the youths of today, except as a mere name associated with California's High Sierra. But Robert Pavlik has done an admirable job in bringing to light Clyde's extraordinary life. The word "unique" is often used inappropriately, but after you read this book I would wager that you can't think of a better word for this prodigious individual. In an obituary for Clyde in 1973, his friend Tom Jukes captured the essence of the man in a few words: "[He] had lived as every alpinist wants to live, but as none of them dare to do....When he died, I felt that an endangered species had become extinct....He was large, solitary, taciturn, and irritable—like the North Palisade in a thunderstorm, and he could also be mellow and friendly, like the afternoon sun on Evolution Lake."

Clyde's name was familiar to all Sierra mountaineers in my youth. You couldn't turn a page of Hervey Voge's 1954 book, *A Climber's Guide to the High Sierra,* without a reference to a Clyde first ascent. I exaggerate slightly, for the master spent much of his time in the central Sierra, or its south, mostly ignoring the Yosemite region, perhaps too tame for him. Most striking of all in Voge's guidebook was the fact that so many of Clyde's ascents were done solo, this in an age when few people roamed the High Sierra, no rescues were possible, and a broken leg away from a popular trail meant an agonizing death. No search-and-rescue teams, no helicopters, no cell phones. A different age, one that Pavlik captures beautifully.

Virtually every solo mountaineer today claims that the inner struggle is what makes the endeavor worthwhile—the overcoming of deep-set fears with no one to turn to for advice or help. In our hectic life today we are so rarely alone that going solo elicits comments about a person's sanity. Clyde did jokingly refer to his mental health in a letter to an acquaintance in 1925: "I sometimes think I climbed enough peaks this summer to render me a candidate for a padded cell—at least some people look at the matter in that way." But one gets the impression from this book that Clyde was simply a run-of-the-mill loner, undoubtedly with a few repressed demons lurking about, but not a man who tried to sway anyone with his solitary exploits. To him, being alone must have been business as usual.

Aside from Clyde's remarkable first-ascent record, what most captivated me back in the 1960s about the already legendary man was the size of his backpack, described with awe by older campfire raconteurs who had actually seen and hefted these monster loads. Though I was impressed that a human could traipse so casually around the high country with a pack that weighed eighty pounds, I was puzzled by some of the reported contents. An axe? A revolver? Hardback books? Hardback books in Greek? A cast-iron frying pan? This was in the days when we all were "going light," a phrase that a decade earlier had been the partial title of an influential Sierra Club primer. Hearing such stories, I thought Clyde must have been a man from an earlier century, perhaps even an alien. And, in a sense, he was. Surely he must have been appalled, near the end of his life, to see bearded hippies with scantily clad girlfriends strolling casually through the High Sierra with twenty-five-pound packs containing a simple aluminum pot, plastic utensils, huge bags of granola, and near-weightless copies of Hermann Hesse's *Siddhartha*.

I thought I knew much about Norman Clyde's life and times, the "times" being when the High Sierra were, paradoxically, both explored and unexplored. Late in life Clyde stated that he had been most active in that interlude between the pioneers—1860 to 1910—and the technical rock climbers, who arrived in the 1930s to scale the "impossible" cliffs. Reading Pavlik, I discovered new insights. For instance, Clyde was well aware that by 1920 excellent maps existed, that the range was well known, and that most of the highest peaks had been climbed. But "minor" unclimbed peaks—like the exquisite Mt. Huxley and the craggy Deerhorn Mountain—were among the most startling formations of the High Sierra. And Clyde sought these out. A forty-year-old kid let loose in a candy store! As Clyde himself admitted, he was not a great technical climber. He seemed content to seek out beautiful or remote peaks with relatively easy routes and often reported later, in his typical laconic manner, "No sign of previous ascent."

Much though I admired Clyde's mountain skills, I was not a fan of his prose, as Pavlik points out in this book. I thought my hero's words were dry and impersonal, and I still feel this way. Yet I was unaware that he wrote such a phenomenal amount. I now picture him at his typewriter on a snowy winter's day, alone as usual, pecking away, probably with two fingers, thinking of new ways to describe his sublime but rather limited universe.

Clyde's personal life was certainly unsettled. Everyone knew that he could be a curmudgeon and occasionally act rude. I met him only once, in a setting he must have hated: a sporting-goods store in Berkeley where I think he was trying to cadge equipment. I was young and timid and hardly said a word; it was enough to simply gaze upon this aging legend. He certainly behaved himself on this brief encounter, but Pavlik has a lot to say about his behavior elsewhere, and this is what makes the book so intriguing. Clyde was no saint and could be downright antisocial at times. With fairness and respect, Pavlik, having done an enormous amount of research over fifteen years, delves into all aspects of Clyde's life.

If Clyde was occasionally cantankerous, he could also be generous. Everyone familiar with High Sierra history knows how Clyde persevered, by himself, in the Minaret Range in 1933, looking for the body of Walter Starr, Jr., long after the other searchers had given up. And I knew of one or two other of his efforts in this regard. Pavlik has discovered, in ancient newspapers and by contacting peripheral people, that Clyde was involved in numerous other unpleasant but necessary searches to locate an overdue hiker or climber. He seems to have had a preternatural ability to know where a missing person would go and how he or she might act. His astonishing knowledge of the natural world helped, so he was quick to see a fresh rockfall scar, for instance, or hear buzzing flies that might indicate a nearby corpse. Clyde was certainly the outstanding human tracker of the High Sierra for many decades.

But Clyde was not simply a California superman, and Pavlik eloquently describes his feats in other regions. Many Sierra aficionados might be unaware of his travels outside the state. An example: Clyde's adventures in Glacier National Park in a matter of weeks during the summer of 1923 are almost unbelievable. In this book you will learn of his endurance and route-finding abilities as he ascended Montana peaks far more complex and dangerous than those in his beloved Sierra. At the time, probably no one in the world was attacking mountains at such a demanding pace. More significantly, this was not some reckless, hotshot kid bent on fame; he was a careful, thirty-eight-year-old climber. Norman Clyde was, without question, a unique individual.

Introduction

The old man sits on the ground, without benefit of a chair to hold him up off the earth. Around him are scattered a lifetime of writings and photographs, remnants of a life lived in the mountains of California and the West. Carefully he reads them, sorts them by subject, and lays their onionskin pages one on top of another. His clothing is neatly pressed, patched, and clean. The collar and cuffs show signs of wear, and the color has faded from the fabric. Perched on his head is a ranger-style campaign hat, a four-dimpled crown surrounded by a wide, flat brim that protects a weathered face from the bright spring sunshine. His sun-scarred hands gently hold the documents before his one good eye, the orb darting over the handwritten pages, his mind traversing the years and miles contained in those few, precious pieces of writing.

The old man is Norman Asa Clyde; the year is 1970. Along with his friend Dick Beach, Norman had returned to his Baker Ranch cabin, above the Owens Valley town of Big Pine, to sort through his belongings. Illness and old age have forced a retreat from his rustic home. When local hoodlums had heard about his absence, they ransacked his cabin in search of a gun collection. The crumpled papers and photographs are among the casualties of their looting spree.

In earlier years Clyde would have begun his day quite differently—perhaps with a walk up the creek to witness the changing weather patterns, or with skis strapped to his feet, to make a daylong exploration of the mountain peaks that surrounded his winter den. Perhaps he would clean and oil one of the many firearms, fresh from a round of target practice. There was always work to be done: repairing a broken camera, organizing fly fishing equipment, splitting and stacking firewood, penning an article for a newspaper or magazine. And there was always the need for physical exertion—a walk, a climb, skiing or snowshoeing in winter, multiday excursions in the summer and fall.

These weren't only pleasant pastimes. Clyde didn't just visit the mountains, he lived in them. As he told a reporter from the *Los Angeles Times*, "I sort of went off on a tangent from civilization and never got back."[1] It was there he made a modest income, writing about his activities in the surrounding region, and guiding those who came to enjoy this spectacular and rugged country. For sixty years he called the Sierra Nevada his home, first as an ardent amateur, and later as a knowledgeable resident and traveler who came to know this range better than any other human being, John Muir included. When old age and infirmity finally forced him to move to the sanitorium in Big Pine, he grudgingly went, but his heart and his mind remained in the high country. Upon returning to his disheveled cabin on Baker Creek, he gathered up papers and photographs, and restored them to order.

In effect, that is the purpose of this book: to pull together the loose threads of one man's life, and to make some sense out of a wide and disparate variety of outlooks, opinions, and viewpoints. Norman Asa Clyde lived for eighty-seven years, coming of age at the end of the nineteenth century and passing away in the third quarter of the twentieth. He learned his skills and practiced his mobility before the age of the automobile, and he lived to see modern-day explorers walk on the moon.

During his lifetime he explored and ascended hundreds of peaks in the mountain ranges of western North America, from Mt. Robson in the Canadian Rockies to El Picacho del Diablo in Baja California. He honed his outdoor skills over a lifetime. He was remarkably self-sufficient and skilled at a variety of tasks, including not only rock climbing and mountaineering but skiing, snowshoeing, fishing, hunting, axemanship, and mountain rescue. Clyde was more than just a mountain explorer. He was an educated man with a keen intelligence and a probing mind. He was well-read, and knowledgeable in a broad spectrum of disciplines—in the arts and humanities as well as the natural sciences. A prolific author, he wrote many articles for the popular press and for mountain journals. And, contrary to popular belief, he was not a hermit, and in the winter season could often be found in the Los Angeles or San Francisco Bay regions, visiting with friends, replenishing his supply of reading material, and planning new excursions. He could also be volatile, his anger and frustration erupting in unpredictable ways that had serious consequences for the strong-willed individualist.

In his biography in *Who's Who in America*, Norman Clyde described himself as an "expert on high altitude flora and fauna (Hudsonian and Arctic Alpine zones of the Sierra Nevada), geological history and structure of mountain ranges of Western U.S., ski mountaineering, classical scholar, linguist."[2] He could have added author, fisherman, teacher, mountain guide, rescuer, and recluse to the list. His unlikely mix of interests and accomplishments reflected a lifetime effort to combine bookish scholarship with wilderness experience, a love of learning with a zealous need for the strenuous life. This mix of ideas and action was the culmination of his lineage combining with opportunity and open space in the New World.

Among climbers and skiers his legend has outdistanced him; among the general population he has been forgotten. Clyde's contributions to the exploration and description of the Sierra Nevada and to the field of mountaineering have been important and long-ranging, and deserve to be known by a wider audience. He was the first person to ascend more than one hundred and thirty peaks throughout western North America, literally standing where no other human being had ever been. He eventually climbed more than one thousand peaks in his lifetime, some several times over. He had a deep and abiding love of the outdoors, fostered at a young age in the woods of western Pennsylvania and Canada. As a teacher he shared his love of the natural world with others. His exploits as a searcher for lost climbers include some of the most dramatic stories of tragedy, triumph, and heroism that have ever taken place in the annals of California history. And, as a pioneer of a then obscure endeavor better known in Europe than in the United States, his record of accomplishments and his promotion of the sport bears examination.

Clyde lived in a world of dazzling granite and glacial ice, deep blue sky and ominously towering thunderheads. He was often alone in this rugged world with only the sound of the wind, his boots on rock and snow, and his slow, steady breathing. He left behind some weathered notes in makeshift summit cairns, his articles and photos, numerous entries in various climbing guides, and tangible memories among a number of friends and acquaintances. This is the story of Norman Clyde, mountaineer, nature writer, and guide.

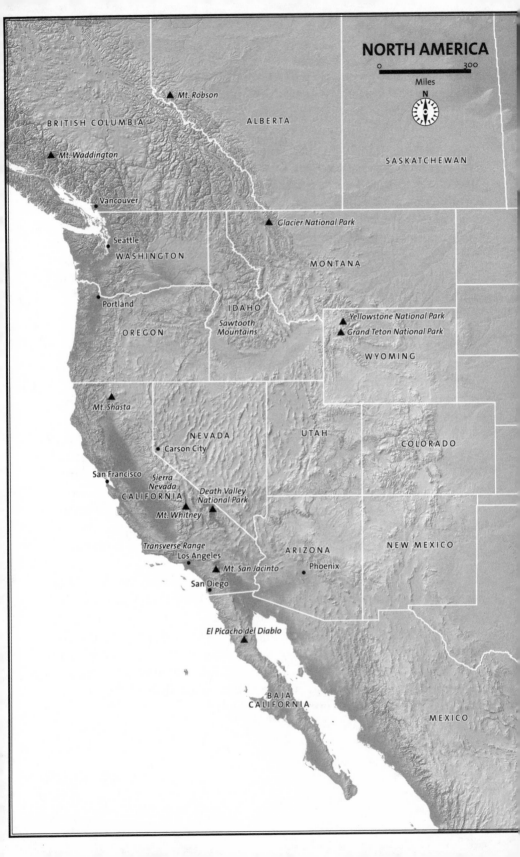

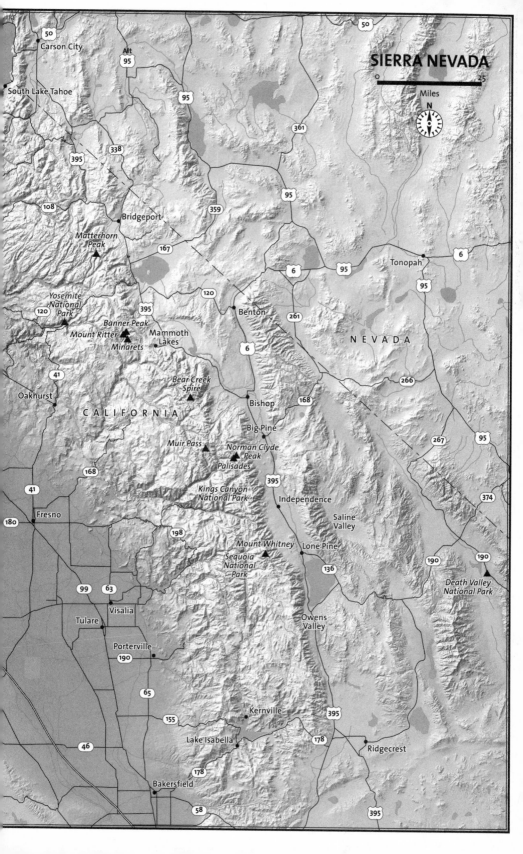

SIERRA NEVADA

0   25
Miles

N

Carson City   50

50

South Lake Tahoe   Alt
                                         95

                              95

                                                  361

                                         95

                        395
              338

108

                                         359
          Bridgeport

                    167   6
     Matterhorn
       Peak   Tonopah

                                        120   6   95

              Yosemite   Benton   95
              National   261
       120   Park   395
                   Banner Peak   N E V A D A
     Mount Ritter
              Minarets   Mammoth   6
                           Lakes

          41
                    Bear Creek   266
                      Spire

   Oakhurst   Bishop   168
        C A L I F O R N I A
                                        Big Pine
                    Muir Pass   267
                      Norman Clyde   95
              168   Peak
                       Palisades   374
          41
                      Kings Canyon   395
                      National Park   Independence

   180   Fresno   190
                                                  Saline
                    198   Valley
                              Mount Whitney   190
                           Sequoia   Lone Pine
                           National   Death Valley
                             Park   136   National Park

          99   63   Owens
                   Visalia   Valley

     Tulare

          Porterville
              190

              65

                    155   Kernville   395

          46   Lake Isabella   178
                                                        Ridgecrest
                    178
          Bakersfield

              58   395

CHAPTER 1

Seeking Out the Wild Places: Family, Boyhood, and Youth

Norman Asa Clyde was a descendant of Irish and American parents who had known hardship and deprivation firsthand. His father, Charles Clyde, was born in Antrim County, Northern Ireland, on May 9, 1856. By that time Ireland had long been in the grip of grinding poverty and food shortages that left more than one and a half million people dead or dying, with an equal number fleeing its shores for the New World. Charles Clyde's parents would soon follow, immigrating to the United States at the beginning of the Civil War. They did not believe in education; they were rug weavers and descended from a line of shipbuilders. Prior to immigrating to Ireland, the Clydes had lived in Scotland and may even be descendants of the Bruce clan, a royal family that fought for Scotland's independence from England.

Norman's mother, Sarah Isabelle Purvis ("Belle") was a native of Glade Mills, Pennsylvania, twenty-five miles north of Pittsburgh, where she was born on November 24, 1863. The Purvises were also of Irish descent but had long been established in America. Her ancestor John Watt was born in Ireland and had immigrated to the colonies in 1773. He served in the Continental Army as a Private Fourth Class under Captain Brisbane in Lancaster County, Pennsylvania. Several years later he fought in the Westmoreland Land Company Militia against the Indians.

Charles and Belle were married in Butler in 1884, later moving to Philadelphia, where their first son, Norman Asa, was born on April 8, 1885.[1] Eight more children would be added to the Clyde clan over the years: two brothers and four sisters survived into adulthood, with one child dying of typhoid and one of tuberculosis. As the eldest son, it was expected of Norman to look after his younger siblings, and to

shoulder much of the burden of helping with the daily chores: hauling water, chopping wood, filling the coal bins for cooking and heat,
and tending to the flocks of chickens and geese that every household
raised for eggs and meat.

Charles Clyde supported his family as a Reformed Presbyterian minister of the Covenantor sect. Such a life would have been
devoted to Bible study, hard work, and few luxuries. Members of the
Reformed Protestant Church (including the Covenantors) eschewed
modern conveniences and big cities because they were deemed to
have a corrupting influence on the moral character of its members;
hence, the Clydes lived at the very margins of civilization, wresting a
living from near-wilderness conditions while bringing the teachings of
Jesus Christ to their backwoods neighbors. Charles flitted from church
to church, seldom staying for more than a year at any one location.
Norman was three when the family moved to Northwood, Ohio; at
the age of twelve he was uprooted to Lochiel Township, Glengarry
County, Ontario, Canada, where they lived in the country, eighty
miles from Ottawa. For the next five years Norman reveled in the
outdoor life of the Laurentian region, hunting and fishing and being
home-schooled by his father, an energetic scholar who taught his son
the Classics in their original Greek and Latin, as well as German,
Spanish, and French. Young Norman would later pick up a book of
Portuguese and learn the language on his own.

Charles Clyde died of pneumonia in Brodie, Ontario, on December
7, 1901, at the age of forty-six. He had contracted blood poisoning as
a result of a cut sustained while repairing the church's stained glass
windows. His passing left sixteen-year-old Norman in charge of the
family. From what little we know of Clyde's early life and his later
years, it was not a role that he relished. Being thrust into a position
of responsibility at such an age is difficult for any child, let alone one
for whom domestic chores and younger siblings were the cause of
strife and irritation. In addition, he appears to have inherited almost
all of his father's wanderlust; with one exception, the rest of his family stayed close to home during their adult lives. Following Charles
Clyde's death, the family stayed on in Canada for two more years,
eventually returning to western Pennsylvania to be closer to Belle's
family.

Norman's lack of formal education did not hamper his quest for
knowledge. Prior to enrolling in Geneva College, a small liberal arts
school in Beaver Falls, Pennsylvania, he had to make up work that was

deemed essential to his education. Knowledge was an important commodity to the entire Clyde clan. All seven of the surviving brothers and sisters attended college, and five earned at least an A.B. degree, which was highly unusual for the time. They each attended Geneva College while working to support themselves and their family. Sisters Sarah, Clara, Grace, and Eva all became teachers. Brother John had two years of college, and brother Arthur became a very popular high school teacher and coach in Morgantown, West Virginia. According to Norman's niece, Vida Brown, "The two [Norman and Arthur] were always wrestling; their mother couldn't control them, they were always going at each other's throats."[2] Although a rough-and-tumble relationship between brothers is not uncommon, the intensity illustrates their commonly shared competitive nature and focused determination.

Following his makeup work, Norman pursued a degree in the Classics. He was on the staff of the *Geneva Cabinet*, the college's magazine, and had two poems and several articles published therein. One poem, "A Winter Sunrise," is worth reprinting here:[3]

The winter night has fled, and rosy morn
Has risen joyfully. An hour ago
The mounting sun, just passing the horizon,
Silvered the tall and silent pines, which rise
Above the eastern woods. It was a time
Of most impressive solemness. The gray
Twilight brooded over everything;
The long white slopes of snow enveloped fields,
The frozen lake and the old majestic woods.
The stars had disappeared; the sinking moon
Shone pallid through the bars of the western wood;
The clouds collected round the rising sun;
Shining gorgeously in gold and red.
It seemed to be a scene of grandeur scarce
Of earth; the silence and starry host
Which glittered in myriads through all the night,
Now sinking away into the depths of space;
The sun uprising slowly, silently
And sending forth the dawn upon the earth.
All this o'erpowered the mind with wonder and
Astonishment at Nature's majesty
And endless harmony. So ever it is

Around us beauties and sublimities
Numberless, wrap us in their embrace,
Had we only the eyes to behold them.[4]

Clyde's poem is interesting for what it can tell us about the author
at this stage of his life. It illustrates an intimate knowledge of the natural landscape that surrounded him, as well as a love of the outdoors.
The poem emphasizes the beauty of nature without creating a human
presence to alter or dilute the scene. The speaker also chides those
who are not aware of their surroundings, in effect dismissing them
for a lack of sensitivity and awareness. Clyde's poetry and world view
shared similar themes and outlooks with those of another native Penn-
sylvanian who later settled on the California coast. The poet Robinson
Jeffers studied the Classics, as well as forestry and medicine, and later
applied his wide knowledge of human history and the natural world
to his own powerful writings where he often, like Clyde in this poem,
avoids an anthrocentric view of the world.

Throughout his college career Clyde took to the outdoors for
respite from his schoolwork and other responsibilities. He liked to play
football, explore caves in the surrounding Beaver Valley, and climb to
the top of the nearby hills. In a *Geneva Cabinet* article titled "College
Recreation" he wrote about one of his "customary rambles" in the
local hills, describing a beautiful autumn day: "As the author gazed at
the lovely spectacle, it occurred to his mind how little we know of the
scenes of beauty which nature constantly spreads before us. It cannot
be that the aspects of nature around us are not inspiring. The com-
monest of landscapes has something of interest to the watchful eye at
any season of the year....Emerson says, 'The moral sensibility which
makes Edens and Tempes so easily, may not always [be] found, but
the material landscape is never far off.' But the country around us, far
from being what might be called tame and devoid of interest, is quite
picturesque. The hills skirting the Beaver form many striking views,
there are numbers of romantic ravines in the vicinity, and the woods
are not without beauty..."[5] He goes on to remind his fellow students
to take advantage of the great wealth of natural beauty that surrounded their small community, in order to see "what majestic beauties daily wrap us in their bosom."

By June 1909, at the age of twenty-four, Clyde had completed his
studies and was awarded the A.B. degree from Geneva. He wasted no
time in bidding his family farewell, and set out for the West. Although

he would remain in touch with his family, and occasionally travel back to visit, he would never return to live in the East. Even though the frontier had disappeared from the American West, there still remained large expanses of wilderness sufficient to challenge the hardiest of outdoorsmen. And, in the wake of Frederick Jackson Turner's 1893 proclamation of the end of the frontier, there were numerous groups and individuals who championed the outdoor life for physical, spiritual, and moral reasons. The growth of the Sierra Club in California, the popularity of the Boone and Crockett Club and the Appalachian Climbing Club in the eastern United States, and, after the turn of the century, the importation of the Boy Scouts from Great Britain all contributed to the zeal for outdoor life. Popular writers, including John Muir, John Burroughs, and John Van Dyke, extolled the virtues of the wilderness of mountain, forest, and desert. Their works found a kindred spirit in Norman Clyde.

Clyde was enormously influenced by John Muir's writings, especially *The Mountains of California* (1894). It is a collection of Muir's essays that had previously appeared in various magazines and one newspaper, and which Muir himself had selected for inclusion in his first published book. Muir wrote an overview of the Sierra Nevada especially for this volume. *The Mountains of California* is considered by many of Muir's admirers to be his finest book.[6] Its presence in 1894, two years after the founding of the Sierra Club, satisfied a growing interest in the Sierra Nevada, and mobilized individuals to take a greater interest in conservation issues.

There are other parallels between the two men. As with Clyde, Muir was a Celtic native (from Scotland) who immigrated to the United States with his family at a young age, settling in the upper Midwest state of Wisconsin. Both came from households where religion was a dominant theme in their lives: Muir's father was a Calvinist Presbyterian and lay minister. It may be safely assumed that at least some of the strict regimen and harsh discipline that had been visited upon John Muir was also the realm of Charles Clyde's firstborn son. Self-reliance was an integral and indispensable characteristic of immigrants to North America who chose (or could afford) to live outside of the tenements of the Eastern seaboard and the Midwestern manufacturing centers. It was a characteristic of the Muir family, and the Clyde family as well.

Although both men hailed from religious parents, they each rejected Judeo-Christian morals and teachings and embraced an earlier (and universal) moral code, better known as the Golden Rule: to do unto others as one would have others do unto himself. This also means that one should respect the other person's right to live as they see fit, without undue interference from outside forces, and in turn, to expect the same from others. That they lived in a time and place where they could be relatively free of encumbrances, be they governmental, social, or religious, enabled them to live their lives with a freedom once associated with frontier America.

Following in Muir's footsteps

Norman wanted to travel; westward was the course of empire, and the direction and destination of Norman Clyde. Lacking the money to travel directly to California, he worked his way across the United States. Train travel was probably his means of transport, as automobiles were still in their infancy and interstate highways nonexistent.

Although he lacked the financial means to make his way across the country, he did not lack for intelligence or ingenuity. His years as head of the Clyde household following his father's death gave him a depth and maturity far beyond his twenty-four years. He possessed an extraordinary physique and a brilliant mind, so that he could always find work with his hands as well as his head.

Following his graduation from Geneva College, Clyde landed a job aboard a Great Lakes steamship, bound for Duluth, Minnesota. Such a job would move him several hundred miles west in short time and put some much needed money in his pocket. He also cited a "'[Francis] Parkman' like love of nature in her wilder and more imposing aspects" as his chief reason for plying the chilly waters of the interior. In his account, written for the *Geneva Cabinet*, he lovingly describes the journey in the late summer and early fall of 1909, as the hardwoods began to turn and the first snows dusted the forests of pine, spruce, hemlock, and fir. Clyde found Lake Superior to be his favorite: "its dark waters, almost ice-cold even in mid-summer, stirred usually by breezes, tossed wildly sometimes by storms together with the cool, pure, refreshing atmosphere, fill one with delight."

During the return journey from Duluth, he was witness to (and almost victim of) the ferocity of Superior's storms. Assigned to the duty of midnight watchman, mountainous seas broke over him as the vessel pitched and rocked. Clyde "found himself grasping the railing and leaning over the leeward side of the boat with a votive offering for Neptune or whatever deity presides over Superior waters." He managed to make his way to his forward post on the bow of the ship, a distance of seventy-five yards from where he came on deck. Clyde reported, "As the writer reached his point of lookout on the bridge, above the pilot-house, in the bow of the boat, the gale was shrieking through the rigging, flapping the canvas around the bridge, and carrying the spray of the foaming waves high into the air. The vessel plunged and lurched, now a wave breaking over her weather-side, then her lee gunwale rocking to the water's edge. In spite of driving snow, flying spray and plunging boat the author remained at his post and experienced a grim pleasure and exultation in the raging elements....For three days, except for short intervals, we had gales, sleet, snow and rain. Still it was a magnificent sight when it temporarily cleared off to watch the myriads of black tossing waves on every side, rising and falling, their crests breaking into snow-white foam." The crew, almost all experienced sailors, suffered from motion sickness and deep fear of the ship sinking from the battering it was taking from the tempest.

By the time the ship reached Chicago, Clyde had "earned the ill-will of the captain, [and] had the good fortune to get discharged." He disembarked and stayed with a former Geneva classmate while exploring the Second City and sitting in on lectures at the University of Chicago. Clyde enjoyed auditing the classes but found the school itself a dull place in comparison with his alma mater. "One hundred Geneva students make as much stir as 3500 Chicago ones. There seems to be little college spirit, class spirit or any spirit at all except that of study. A very high standard of scholarship prevails, yet there is nothing else to do." Clyde signed off his "tedious remarks" with the sobriquet "Cyclops," a nickname he was apparently well known by at Geneva. In Greek mythology Cyclops was the one-eyed monster of tremendous strength who unleashed unmitigated terror against its enemies. Exactly what earned him this colorful title is not known. However, it could be inferred that the name applied to any number of possible traits, including his strength and stamina, single-minded focus, and hot temper.[7]

Following his stint as a merchant seaman, Clyde became a schoolteacher for the next eighteen years. His academic background prepared him well, and he no doubt chose it in part for the freedom it would afford him to spend time in the mountains during the summer months. Clyde worked his way across the United States as a high school teacher in North Dakota, Utah, and Florence, Arizona, where he arrived to teach school with a Colt handgun at his side. Clyde admitted that the locals were probably taken aback by a schoolteacher wearing a firearm. Clyde was merely relishing his arrival in the American West, playing the role of the lone stranger riding into town, complete with shooting irons.[8] He spent the summer at the University of Wisconsin–Madison (John Muir's alma mater), and another summer working on a cattle ranch in Utah.[9]

A picture postcard written by Clyde to his mother on June 30, 1910, is an early expression of his proclivity for the mountains. The card was postmarked at Camp Curry, in Yosemite Valley. He wrote: "Dear Mother—I have come up to the Yosemite to spend some time. I have seen the Wawona Big Trees and made a wonderful knapsack trip into the High Sierras in which I climbed the highest mountains this region. Sincerely, N. Clyde."[10] Later, Norman wrote to his mother from Giant Forest in Sequoia National Park: "Dear Mother—Arrived here several days ago and shall leave in several more. This is a wonderful place for trees…thousands of great sequoias. Shall be going to McLoud [sic] a town in the northern part of the state near Mt. Shasta. Your son, N. Clyde."[11] His natural attraction to the mountains, a strong interest in the Big Trees, and a matter-of-fact statement that he "climbed the highest mountains in the region" all point to his future as a mountaineer.

Clyde seemed to be seeking out the wild places that Muir had described many years earlier. His profession enabled him to spend summers rambling along the great backbone of the Golden State, from the Tehachapis to Mt. Shasta. Clyde taught school in McCloud and in nearby Weaverville, enabling him to hike, climb, explore, and restore himself in wild places.[12]

The desire for additional schooling pulled Clyde back to civilization, at least temporarily. Following his stint in Northern California he relocated to the San Francisco Bay Area, where he taught at Lowell High School and attended U.C. Berkeley from 1911 to 1913.[13] He later returned to Berkeley for the 1923-24 school year to pursue postgraduate studies in English. Following several years of study he lacked only one course and a thesis for completing his master's degree. He refused to participate in a "Dramas of the Romance Languages"

8

course, insisting that Italian plays should be read in Italian, French dramas in French, neither one in English; and he could not see the sense in writing a thesis that, once it was filed on the library shelf, may never be read or referred to again.[14] He left the university without completing the degree, but then, perhaps his reason for attending graduate school in the first place was not for the degree but for the pleasure it gave him to be back in school. He could read in six different languages, and his interests were diverse. During his career as a teacher and principal he taught history, science, and Latin, and so his main motivation for attending school may have been for the sheer pleasure and enjoyment, without thought of or concern for upward mobility in his teaching career.[15]

Love and Loss

One of Clyde's most private and painful experiences in his life was his brief marriage. On June 15, 1915, he was wed to Winifred May Bolster, a tall, slender, attractive woman with thick dark hair. She was born in New York on May 1, 1890, to William and Margaret V. Bolster. The family had moved to California when Winifred was twelve years old, settling in Pasadena.

Very little is known of Norman and Winnie's acquaintance, courtship, and marriage. It is believed that they met while they were students, Norman at U.C. Berkeley and Winnie in nursing school in Oakland. They married in Pasadena, at the Lincoln Avenue Methodist Church. Winnie was attended to by her sister, Roberta "Byrd" Austin; her mother was a witness. Following the nuptials the couple honeymooned in Santa Barbara before returning to Oakland, where they took up residence. Norman was teaching and Winnie was working as a nurse in a tuberculosis hospital. It was there that she herself caught the dreaded disease, commonly known as "consumption."

The couple relocated to Pasadena, near Winnie's family, and she was placed in the La Vina Sanitarium of Altadena. She suffered for four years and died at age twenty-eight on Valentine's Day, 1919. She was buried at Mountain View Cemetery three days later.[16] According to Winifred's nephew Walter Bolster, Winifred's mother and sister blamed Norman for Winnie's sickness; perhaps it was Winifred's desire to have a career, maybe it was the young couple's tenuous financial status that required a double income. Whatever the reason, it is likely that Winifred had been exposed to TB while working as a nurse, perhaps even prior to their courtship and marriage. The bitterness and vituperations caused a permanent rift between the Clyde and Bolster clans. Prior to the tragic turn of events, Norman and his in-laws had gotten along well; they enjoyed family get-togethers and he even took his brother-in-law on hikes in the nearby mountains. Following Winifred's death, Norman left Pasadena and never contacted any Bolster family member again.[17]

Norman must have been devastated. He would rarely speak of his wife, or of the fact that he had been married, to anyone, not even his closest friends. One of the few people to have elicited this information from Clyde was Walt Wheelock, editor and publisher of *Close Ups of the High Sierra*. While Wheelock was conducting research for *Close Ups* he visited Clyde several times. As a retired Glendale Police officer who had worked on the force for twenty-seven years, Wheelock was successful in extracting information from his subject, even on topics as sensitive as his all-too-brief marriage. This bit of information came as a shock to many people, who always assumed that Clyde was simply a bachelor who jealously guarded his freedom. There is also that reserved—some might say suppressed—quality characteristic of both his time and upbringing, embodied in the prevailing attitude and outlook that pain and hardship is a part of one's life. Outward displays of grief or dismay were strictly off-limits, especially to men. The bottling up of these intense feelings of loss and privation manifested themselves in other, more sinister and sometimes destructive ways. His marriage had a tremendous impact on his life, and would shape his future relationships, especially with women.

CHAPTER 2

The Pack that Walked like a Man: Early Climbs, 1910–1924

Norman Clyde came west to explore and experience wilderness. His chosen career of teaching enabled him to spend his summers scrambling on the peaks and rambling among the heights. His postcard to his mother in 1910 indicated that he had come to California, and the Sierra Nevada, to "climb the highest mountains in this region." Although no other record exists regarding the specific peaks that he climbed, that may be attributable to the one of several possible reasons: perhaps he simply did not record his name in the summit registers, or there was no register available, or the record has since been lost.[1] And, the loss of his wife both freed him to pursue his passion and impelled him on to an almost furious drive to climb.

Clyde himself stated that 1914 was the first year that he began a regimented program of climbing in the Sierra.[2] Yosemite appears to have been his training ground, and of the eleven climbs that he made in 1914 (for which there are records), eight of them were in Yosemite: Mt. Lyell, Unicorn Peak, Cathedral Peak, Mt. Dana, Mt. Gibbs, Foerster Peak, Electra Peak, and Mt. Parker. Three of the eight—Electra, Parker, and Foerster—were first ascents; his routes up all three are classified as "Class 2," which means that they can be climbed in hiking boots, with an occasional use of the hands. Clyde also made his first ascent that year of Mt. Whitney, the highest peak in the continental United States.[3]

Joining the Sierra Club introduced Clyde to the mountains that would later become his home, provided him with companionship and, later, a paycheck, and offered him an outlet for his writings. The club was formed in 1892 by a group of prominent San Francisco Bay Area leaders, who elected John Muir their first president. Two of the aims of the club suited Clyde well: "To explore, enjoy, and render accessible the mountain regions of the Pacific Coast; [and] To publish authentic information concerning them..."[4] William Colby, working in conjunction with Muir, started the popular annual summer outings for members in 1901. That first summer in the Sierra, ninety-six club members traveled to Tuolumne Meadows to explore and enjoy the high country.

The phrase "render accessible" held particular importance for mountain explorers in the late nineteenth and early twentieth centuries. Getting to Yosemite wasn't the leisurely journey in air-conditioned comfort that it is today. Travel was time-consuming, expensive, uncomfortable, and exhausting. Trains transported visitors from the urban centers to small towns like Merced, where they boarded stages or, after 1907, a narrow-gauge railroad that took them to El Portal, gateway to the park. The early wagon roads were steep and narrow, choked with dust during the summer and impassable during and after winter storms. Most visitors to Yosemite restricted themselves to the developed areas of the park—Yosemite Valley, Glacier Point, and the Mariposa Grove—leaving vast tracts of high country to the occasional wilderness traveler and the infrequent Army patrols. Following the Army's departure in 1913 and the advent of the private automobile, tourism increased dramatically, with a subsequent demand for improved access and accommodations. Those hardy individuals who wanted to escape the campgrounds and hotels on the valley floor found their kindred spirits in other Sierra Club members, who preferred to explore the unpopulated and alluring backcountry.

Clyde's climbing activities over the next few years approximated those of a motivated and energetic novice. In 1916 he made his first ascent of Mt. Shasta, which he climbed eleven more times during his life, including three times in four days.[5] The following summer he was living in Southern California and climbing Mt. San Jacinto with fellow Sierra Club members.[6] Winifred Clyde's illness kept her active husband close to home, and although there is no record of his climbing activities in the few years prior to her death in 1919, he no doubt frequented the nearby San Gabriel Mountains, which he could see from the front of his house on North Mentor Avenue in Pasadena.

Following his wife's death Clyde sought solitude and comfort in the mountains. The Kings-Kern Divide region of the southern Sierra was the target of Clyde's climbing activities for the 1919 season. During that summer he climbed Mt. Brewer, East Vidette, Mt. Tyndall, and

University Peak, and made two ascents of Mt. Whitney and a second ascent of Mt. Ritter to the north. Clyde was exploring the range from south to north, beginning to fill in some of the voids on his own internal map of the range.

The following year Clyde joined the Sierra Club on their trek from Yosemite Valley to the Evolution Basin. He spent several days in the Clark Range, where he climbed Mt. Clark, Gray Peak, Red Peak, and Merced Peak, and recorded a first ascent of Triple Divide Peak.[7] During this period Clyde secured his reputation for being well prepared on wilderness excursions. He was a few days behind the other club members as they made their way from Yosemite Valley south, so he stocked up with ample provisions prior to setting out. At Camp Curry he stopped to weigh his pack, which at seventy-five pounds was more than half of his own weight of one hundred forty pounds. The following evening Clyde met up with a backcountry survey crew, who were impressed with the large load that the redheaded teacher was toting. They pressed an additional twenty pounds of provisions on the unsuspecting hiker, just to see if he could take it. Clyde realized some miles down the trail that he had been made the butt of their joke; however, not being one to pass up free food, he doubtless made good use of the supplies.[8] In later years he became known as "the pack that walks like a man."[9] Traveling south along the John Muir Trail, Clyde recorded a first ascent of Mt. Huxley on July 15.[10] On the same trip he also climbed (from north to south) Mt. Woodworth, Observation Peak, Mt. Clarence King, Black Mountain, Dragon Peak (a possible first ascent), Mt. Gould, Mt. Rixford, and Mt. Bago.[11]

A few years later Clyde journeyed north, stopping first at Mt. Shasta. He set a record for the ascent of the volcanic peak, climbing from Horse Camp (8,000 ft. elevation) to the summit (14,161 ft.) in three hours and seventeen minutes on July 3, 1923. Not satisfied with this effort, he again ascended the peak on July 5, making the climb in two hours and forty-three minutes, speeding up the 35-degree slope at a rate of 37.5 feet per minute. The *Mount Shasta Herald* claimed that Clyde "now holds the undisputed record for climbing Mount Shasta."

In late August local climbing guide Barney McCoy claimed to have summited the peak in a record-busting two hours and seventeen minutes. The Sierra Club disputed the claim, refusing to overturn Clyde's record. Clyde himself offered his opinion on the matter to William Colby and fellow Sierra Club member M. Hall McAllister that "[I] do not believe for a minute that he [McCoy] ever made the climb in the time mentioned. The snow is off and his record is next to impossible."[12]

From Shasta Clyde went on to Glacier National Park in Montana. In 1923 he spent almost five weeks in its backcountry. At the end of his trip, he resolved to climb one more peak, Mt. Wilbur, thought at the time to be unscalable. Following a careful study of the peak, first from the summit of nearby Grinnell Mountain and them from the veranda of the Many Glacier Hotel, he concluded that the peak could be climbed from the east. A fellow climber and possible companion, Mr. Elrod, conferred with Clyde but concluded that the chimneys Clyde was thinking of climbing were "impossible to scale." Clyde came to a different conclusion, and set out the next morning for the summit.

Heavy clouds obscured the top half of the mountain as he started his approach. Skirting Iceberg Lake, he scaled the walls rising above the icy water and there encountered an impassable rock face. As the clouds lifted and the afternoon wore on, he began to improvise a route. He scrambled over the tough diorite and worked his way up the chimneys and the ridge between them. Using both his prodigious strength and methodical style he gradually made his way to the summit. As he rested he took in the panoramic views that he was now amply familiar with, and replayed in his mind both the climb he had just completed as well as those of the past several weeks. Following a well-deserved rest, Clyde began to build a summit monument to the memory of Dr. Frank B. Wynn, a fellow climber who had lost his life on nearby Mt. Siyeh. Clyde wrote (in the third person) that he

> worked lustily, but the sun was now low in the west, and if darkness should overtake him he [Clyde] would be unable to make the descent. Having erected a cairn some seven feet in height, he cautiously descended as the shadows of evening crept gradually over the mountain. On the following morning the monument could be seen with the naked eye from the veranda of Many Glacier Hotel, and the precipitous form of Mount Wilbur did not seem to tower so defiantly across the lucid waters of the lovely Lake McDermott.[13]

His exploits in Glacier at that time were so remarkable that they warranted a press release from the National Park Service:

HE CLIMBS A MOUNTAIN A DAY DURING 36 DAYS
OF HIKING, ESTABLISHING A WORLD RECORD

Washington, D.C., Sept.—Norman Clyde, 38, a small-town
schoolmaster of Weaverville, California, climbed 36 mountain
peaks, one each consecutive day, during his recent camping
hike through Glacier National Park. On the summits of eleven
of those 36 mountains he failed to find evidence of any one else
ever having scaled them.

This amazing feat in mountain climbing, it is believed, sets
a world's record. So far as information in the possession of the
Bureau of National Parks is concerned, no single mountaineer
ever accomplished any such feat as this.

Clyde is a member of the Sierra (a mountaineer) Club of
San Francisco. He left Glacier Park and returned to California
August 25th, the day after he scaled the last of the 36 mountains.
This was Mt. Wilbur, 9,283 feet, which he regarded as the most
difficult of them all. He left as his cairn, on this peak, a monument to the late Dr. Wynn, of Indianapolis, Indiana, a mountain
climber of national repute, who had made unsuccessful attempts
to scale Mt. Wilbur.

This monument Clyde heaped up in three hours. He used
loose Argyllite rocks he found on the summit, and built a pyramid seven feet high and six feet at the base. Through field glasses
this mountain peak monument is visible to tourists from the
veranda at Many Glacier Hotel.

Following are the other ten of the 36 mountains Clyde climbed,
upon which he failed to find any record of previous ascents: Nor-
ris, Mt. Logan and also a pinnacle west of Logan, Almost-A-Dog
Mountain, Citadel Mountain, Fusillade Mountain, main peak of
Mount Rockwell, Mount Clements, Avalanche Peak, and Iceberg
Peak.[14]

While the Office of Public Information of the National Park Service obviously delighted in Clyde's accomplishments, using them to
promote the park, Clyde felt compelled to set the record straight, even
if it was only for his own records. A penciled notation on the press
release, written in Clyde's handwriting, states that the information
was "not absolutely accurate. Probably a world record as far as solo
climbing is concerned."[15]

The summer of 1924 found Clyde back in Montana and Glacier National Park, where he climbed Mt. Merritt.[16] It was yet another peak in a series of first ascents in Glacier, and one of nineteen on whose summit he stood that summer. After two seasons of climbing in the park he had ascended virtually every formidable and worthwhile peak that the region had to offer, with the exception of Kinnerly Peak, which he would climb for the first time (and for yet another first ascent) in 1937.[17]

At the end of each summer, he would return to California. As the summer of '24 came to a close, Clyde began a new assignment in the town of Independence, east of the Sierra Nevada in Owens Valley. He brought with him a decade of teaching experience, a love of the mountains, and a dark and disturbing side of his personality that would emerge in the rain shadow of the Range of Light.

CHAPTER 3

A Hell of a Thing to Do: Incident at Independence High School

Norman Clyde had a bad temper. His anger could erupt at the slightest provocation, causing irrational and sometimes dangerous behavior. Former Sierra Club President Richard Leonard recalled an incident in 1930 or '31 when Clyde and fellow mountaineer Bestor Robinson were headed for a climb in Death Valley. Robinson's brother-in-law, Horace Breed, became impatient following the slow-paced Clyde in his car on unpaved dirt roads. Breed passed Clyde, leaving him in a cloud of dust. Clyde became so angry that he produced a revolver and was preparing to shoot Breed for his callous indiscretion. Robinson grabbed the gun away from Clyde, narrowly averting a tragedy.[1]

It was not the first time that Clyde had leveled a weapon against another person. In an undated, unpublished article entitled "My Colt Woodsman," Clyde relates a chilling tale in which he confesses to shooting another man, perhaps killing him. The introductory paragraph of the draft reads:

A hand gun of some sort, provided that its carrier is at least reasonably proficient in its use, is often a convenient [sic] and in case of emergency may even prove a lifesaver. In the mountains and deserts of the west it is rare indeed that one has any occasion to use it against persons. During a considerable number of years of roaming about over them, I have been obliged to do so only once. Had I not, however, on that occasion, a Colt Woodsman and more particularly a Colt 38-40 New Service six gun along with me, it is very difficult to know in what the incident would have culminated. It is very possible that my having a hand gun

17

available and using it for just cause averted certain very serious results: so much so, in fact, that their prevention was far more than worth all the toting of hand guns that I have ever done. There was no law officer to resort to in the affair. I had nothing to depend on to protect two defenseless women, but a hand gun in either hand, and when the menacing party began to shoot, I did likewise with the result that the former was silenced, in very summary fashion.[2]

After the article was typed in draft, Clyde thought better of the passage, drew a line through it, and wrote "omit." What cannot be omitted from any comprehensive story of his life, however, is his volcanic temperament. Was Clyde engaging in some Wild West–style fiction, in order to add color and excitement to his story? There does not appear to be any other record of such a showdown.

The most famous and widely spread story of Clyde's eruptive anger is about when he lost his job as principal of Independence High School. As Neill C. Wilson wrote in a contemporary article, "the high school once had a good, solid sort of principal. And he dealt with his pupils in a good, solid way. But one day one of the older boys took him out in the school yard and offered this good, solid pedagogue a good, solid beating-up, with the result that the school board hired a bigger principal."[3] The school's new principal was Clyde, a serious scholar and a man strong enough to control his rough-hewn students.

Independence is the Inyo County seat, situated in Owens Valley at the base of the eastern Sierra. The valley was largely occupied by grain farmers, orchardists, and their families. They were slowly being driven from farming by the City of Los Angeles, which had been quietly acquiring land and water rights in the valley since 1904. By the time Clyde had arrived in Owens Valley to stay, the tensions between farmers and Los Angeles's Department of Water and Power (DWP) were reaching a flash point. In November of 1924, the same year that Clyde assumed leadership of Independence High, the local citizens of Independence, Manzanar, and Lone Pine seized control of the aqueduct floodgates located near the Alabama Hills, on the valley's west side. They diverted water headed for Los Angeles back to the Owens River, making a symbolic gesture to wrestle control of their lives from politicians and real estate speculators in that distant city. Many valley residents met with financial ruin as their failing farms and businesses were slowly desiccated. It was not an easy time, nor a happy one, in the valley.

Into this high desert town that was struggling to survive came a man who was indifferent to their problems of drought, water diversion, and long-term sustainability. He was a strict disciplinarian hired to do a job: run a school and teach to the best of his knowledge and ability. Whatever economic or political strife the community was experiencing was not his concern. He had no family, owned no land or business, and was not interested in local affairs. He came to Owens Valley to be close to the mountains. On Friday afternoons he would lock the school's doors and head for the high country, returning on Monday morning (and sometimes not until Tuesday) to re-open the school and resume classes. Many people in the valley thought him strange, eccentric; they didn't understand his attraction to the mountains, or why he would want to climb them. After all, they're just there, a constant lurking presence that, sooner or later, everyone took for granted. They could understand going to the mountains to fish, or hunt, or to work in the mines or cut timber, but to hike and climb the more formidable peaks for climbing's sake was a pastime enjoyed by relatively few. To compound the problem, Clyde did not perform the social duties that were thought proper for a school principal to perform—attend social functions, become active in community affairs.

The students also thought him strange for his habit of shooting birds with a BB gun, an activity that, according to Omie Mairs, then a recent graduate and Los Angeles DWP employee, Clyde spent "a lot of time" doing.[4] He was proficient with all sorts of guns—handguns, rifles, shotguns—a skill he no doubt learned while growing up in the mountains and woods of Pennsylvania and Canada.

It was Halloween night, 1928, and Principal Clyde was on patrol at the high school. It was still a relatively new facility, built in 1922, and Clyde was determined to protect the school from the hooligans and rowdies who had committed acts of petty vandalism in the past. Early in the evening a group of students took a casual drive by the school. Omie Mairs was in the front seat of the old touring car; three of his friends were in the rear. As Mairs recalls, Clyde "was in the school itself. And he stepped out on the front porch and he shot the gun, and bang! It sure made a loud noise and I didn't realize where it hit until we drove around. Somebody said, 'well, it hit the car.' So we drove up to the sheriff's office and showed the sheriff where it hit. It had hit right under the rear seat and it went completely through that car....I remember [Sheriff] Tom Hutchinson came out and said, 'well, I'll be darned. That's a hell of a thing to do.' That's all he said, old Tom, he just looked at it for a while and we drove off. We probably went and got some more wine or something....We didn't go up and down the street showing it to people, either. We just drove over there and I guess we were a little frightened. I was. After I saw where the bullet hit, I was a little frightened."[5]

Were the students egging on the hotheaded principal? Perhaps. Was his response extreme? Absolutely. He was an excellent shot, and it has been suggested that he was aiming for a tire, but the fact remains that Clyde's temper got the best of him. He later claimed to have warned the cars away from the building earlier in the evening, something that Mairs did not remember. For years Clyde would staunchly proclaim his innocence, maintaining that he did not shoot at the car, only into the air over their heads.[6]

At the Monday night meeting of the school district trustees, five days later, Clyde presented his resignation for acceptance "at their pleasure." According to the account published in the *Inyo Register*, the trustees' "pleasure happened to be for immediate acceptance, and a warrant was drawn paying Clyde in full to that time."[7]

While some difficulties were brought to an end, others lingered. Clyde was finally free to hike, climb, read, and write without the daily obligations of a full-time career. He had been teaching for fifteen years, and his heart was in the mountains and not in a classroom or an office in the valley. He was now able to embark on a life lived in the open, without all of the attendant responsibilities that a job and family entailed. While there would be many times that Clyde lived hand to mouth, his remarkable constitution enabled him to endure hard physical labor, punishing weather, and months of solitude. One difficulty that grew over time was his animosity and resentment toward the people of Owens Valley, and especially of the town of Independence. Although Omie Mairs claimed that there were no hard feelings toward Clyde, the reverse was not true. For years Clyde harbored ill will toward and a sense of alienation from the people of the valley.[8] That he may have been "framed" remains a distinct possibility, however, the facts have faded with time, and the full truth may never be known.

The challenge remained for Clyde to reconcile his love of mountains and nature with his tempestuous relationships with people. His quick temper seemed at odds with his cool, calculating, and methodical movements on mountainsides. He was able to have a much greater degree of control over his environment when he was in the high country, either alone or with a few close friends and climbing partners, but when he felt pressured or otherwise imposed upon, he would lose patience and sometimes resort to violence. Clyde was smart enough to understand and respect his limits while in the backcountry; he must have realized that in order to maintain his personal freedom and keep from making a serious mistake that could land him in prison he needed to go into a self-imposed exile, become a refugee from society. His sanctuary became the Sierra Nevada.

CHAPTER 4

A Prodigious Climber of Mountains: Close-Ups of Our High Sierra

The question remains, how did Clyde support himself after resigning from the principalship of Independence High School? By all accounts, Clyde led an austere existence. Bookman and fellow mountaineer Ernest Dawson often loaned Clyde money, and as far as Dawson's son Glen knows, his father was always reimbursed. Clyde made Dawson's Book Shop in Los Angeles his personal "post office, storage area, bank, message center, library, and meeting place. He came down from Owens Valley once or twice a year."[1] Clyde's penchant for equipment also meant that he hoarded whatever belongings he had accumulated, with the idea that someday they might come in handy. Norman's old car, a 1926 Chevrolet touring car, was loaded to the top of its cloth tonneau roof with climbing equipment: ropes, ice axes, shoes, packs, pots, pans, and various and sundry personal items. Glen Dawson recalls a mouse living in the car, safe from Norman's baited traps. Clyde had the same effect on the places that he holed up in during the winter. Norman B. Livermore, Jr., recalled renting Clyde a cabin one winter and described the aftermath as "a boar's nest."[2]

Clyde's low standards for personal hygiene also tended to keep people at bay. Around the Owens Valley town of Bishop he was not infrequently referred to as "Filthy McNasty."[3] Sierra Club member Dorothy Leavitt Pepper flatly states, "He would not wash. The same mosquito was on his face for three days. I didn't know for weeks that he was bald. He wore this army hat, and he never took it off. When he did, the top of his head was just as white as milk. The rest of his face was very red. He'd get sunburned and blistered."[4] Of course, being a mountain man did not mean one always had to be unkempt; Clyde could be quite presentable when the time and situation warranted.

The fact of the matter was that his hygiene wasn't just a matter of neglect: he was also at the mercy of the seasons, changing weather, and his own at times rigorous schedule.

Norman was also known for his enormous appetite. He developed something of a reputation as a mooch, inviting himself to partake of others' meals, and then consuming gargantuan portions. Dorothy Pepper recalls, "When I first met him, somebody came along and said, 'Norman, will you have a piece of pie?' He said, 'I don't know. I've had three pieces and I'm pretty well tanked up.' But he reached over and took another piece."[5] Robert Clunie once said, "The only thing I ever hid on him when I saw him coming for dinner was the jellies. You might as well have a bear in camp."[6] Clyde's landlady and owner of Glacier Lodge, Bertha Horine, once tried to fill him up with ham, eggs, and hotcakes, all to no avail. Her food supply and patience gave out before his appetite did. Bob Clunie once succeeded in getting Clyde to say that he'd had "too much to eat," after consuming twelve trout and a gallon of stew.[7] No doubt Clyde later worked off the heavy meal with a hike, climb, or by splitting and stacking a small mountain of firewood.

Other than relying on the generosity of others, Clyde supported himself as a writer. He was nothing if not prolific: the catalog of his writings, housed at the Bancroft Library at the University of California, Berkeley, identify 1,467 articles on many subjects, most of which featured hiking and climbing techniques; rescues; geographical descriptions (canyons, creeks, glaciers, lakes, rivers, meadows, and mountain passes); natural history subjects (bears, bighorn sheep, deer, mountain lions, birds, insects, flowers, and fish); as well as his numerous hobbies, pastimes, and pursuits, including skiing, photography, guns, camping, and mountain craft (e.g., making comfortable camps, building large fires, sanitation, etc.).

Representative titles from the collection include "A Day in May on University Peak," "Consider the Machete," "Unavoidable Hardships—Ignore Them," and "Snow Bound in the Sierra Nevada." If a publisher rejected an article, Clyde would rewrite and edit the article for re-submission. He was published in the *Sierra Club Bulletin*, *Touring Topics* (later called *Westways*), *National Motorist*, *Southern Sierran*, *Boys' Life*, the *Fresno Bee*, and other newspapers, journals, and magazines. The mountaineering articles and knapsack travelogues were unique, as the country he was writing about had rarely been described in such detail, and many of his pieces were accompanied by his own photographs. His articles appealed to both armchair enthusiasts and Sierra Club members alike, especially in an era before climbing guidebooks to the High Sierra were published.

The wellspring for Clyde's writing remained the life he lived in the mountains. The high country was what Clyde wanted all along, and equipped as he was with the skills to survive and thrive there, he did not require large amounts of money. Whether it was writing, guiding, trail building, conducting searches, caretaking remote mountain lodges in winter, or carrying heavy loads for "go-light knapsackers," he could earn enough money to live comfortably. His lifestyle enabled him to do what he most wanted: climb mountains, fish, study the plant and animal life, and come as close to nature as he could.

"If I am going to fall I would prefer to fall straight down"

Even before his resignation from Independence High School, a job that had placed limitations on his time and mobility, Clyde's climbing exploits were not confined to the Sierra Nevada. All of the mountain ranges of western North America seemed to interest him. Following the 1925 season, during which he made fifty-three climbs in the Sierra Nevada (twenty-three of which were first ascents), Clyde traveled north the following summer to Yellowstone National Park with the Sierra Club. After spending a week in the park they headed south to Jackson Hole, Wyoming, where Clyde led two groups of climbers up Grand Teton on July 14 and July 19, 1926, squeezing in a solo climb of Mt. Moran on the 17th. The first party's ascent of Grand Teton, the highest peak in the Teton Range, was a challenge for the group, which included Ernest Dawson, J. O. Downing, Alice Carter, Dottie Baird, and Julie Mortimer.[8]

Clyde served as a route finder, despite the fact that he had never before climbed Grand Teton. Ernest Dawson wrote that the group was armed only with "mis-information gleaned from gas-dispensers, anglers, and resort keepers" who told them to "always take right-hand trails." As a result, they lost four hours of daylight and gained and lost a thousand feet in elevation while making the approach.[9]

Thanks to Clyde's efforts, the party found its way to the base of the climb. Clyde continued to lead the way over some difficult pitches. At one point their narrow ledge disappeared; Dawson stated that if not for Clyde "it is likely that at this point we would have turned back; but at this critical juncture he made a little jump, pulled himself up, and gained the crack above, getting soaked by the icy stream on the way. Worming his way up the crack thirty feet or more, he threw a rope, and one by one the rest of us scrambled up or were pulled to a somewhat safer ledge."[10]

At mid-afternoon the group stood on the summit of Grand Teton, where Clyde observed that "the atmosphere was clear and the view perfect." After a brief rest, the group carefully picked its way down, using only the light of a single candle and an occasional flash of lightning to guide the party through the dark. They arrived back at camp after midnight, concluding a trek that had begun more than nineteen hours earlier.

Later that day Clyde was laying plans for climbing Mt. Moran. He solicited whatever information he could obtain, including advice from the proprietor of the hotel on Jackson Lake, who had made numerous hunting forays into the area. Clyde sought to acquire the necessary equipment for the climb but met with only limited success; an ice axe was nowhere to be found, so he had to settle for a prospector's pick. Depositing his gear in a rented boat, he proceeded to row himself across Jackson Lake, a distance of ten miles. A strong headwind doubled the time it normally took to cross, but Clyde was undeterred. Reaching the far side, he secured the boat, shouldered his pack, and trudged on to meet the mountain.

Clyde sought out a campsite below the glacier, on a steep slope near a spring. He later recalled that below him were "several miniature meadows in which abounded exquisitely tinted lupine, castilleas, and columbines. Far below was the azure expanse of Jackson Lake, and on the southeastern horizon, beyond a diversified area of verdant mountain and plain, loomed the lofty snow-clad range of the Wind River Mountains. Several hundred feet above camp was the glacier, and above that towered the dark, rugged summit of Mount Moran."[11]

Early the next morning Clyde climbed the glacier and scrambled up the crest to the summit. From the top he gazed on Grand Teton, on which he had stood three days earlier. The mountains and plains of Wyoming stretched out all around him. He added his name to those of the eight or nine others who had previously achieved the summit, and went about observing the mountain's geology. He marveled at the presence of a marmot, and wondered how the creature could survive at an elevation of more than 12,000 feet with the sparse vegetation that was present.

The descent was long and tedious. Armed with his prospector's pick, Clyde was forced to descend the steep glacier facing inward, as if climbing down a fifteen-hundred-foot-tall ladder. This experience no doubt reinforced his belief in the importance of proper equipment.

Norman was at the hotel at Moran on July 18 to greet the second party of Sierra Clubbers intent on climbing Grand Teton. Seven men and three women joined Clyde in retracing the route that the first group had followed the previous week. The weather had turned cold, with snow, rain, and hail in place of warm sunshine, and the views were obscured by fog and mist. The group remained stalwart, even giddy, as they joked, "It's a great view up here, anyway. We saw it fine from the lower end, looking up." Neill Wilson wrote, "One hour after his [Clyde's] safe arrival down from Mount Moran, he was taking ten pilgrims again up the Grand Teton, known as the 'Matterhorn of America,' whose steep rocky face forced him at one point to lift all ten of them by ropes. This he did, handling them as nonchalantly as a farmer would handle sacks of barley."[12] After adding their names to the sixty others contained in a glass bottle stashed in the summit cairn, they started down.[13]

Clyde made a few more climbs in the Yellowstone region, including Mt. Sheridan, Hancock Peak, the Trident, and Colter Peak, before moving on to the Beartooth and Absaroka Ranges in Montana. There he made another series of climbs, including Mt. Republic, Grand Mountain, Mt. Zimmer, Glacier Peak, and "several peaks over 10,000 feet on Fox and Goose Ridge."[14] Clyde had his sights set on a peak in the Beartooth Range, Granite Peak, at 12,799 feet the highest mountain in Montana. He spent two rainy weeks in August exploring the region, which also included a first ascent of Silvertop Mountain. Because Granite Peak had only been climbed once, Clyde was having a difficult time securing any information. He couldn't even find a map of the area. Fortunately he met up with a party from Billings who were en route to Granite Peak, and fell in with them.

The five men plotted a path to Granite Peak "through a rough, trailless region....It was sort of no man's land, above timber-line (here about 10,000 feet above sea-level)—a monotonous expanse of broken granite hills, occasionally relieved by an azure rock-bound lake."

Clyde and a "young Swiss" left the group and advanced toward the peak, camping at nightfall in the recesses of Avalanche Lake Basin. The pair struck out at first light for the summit. They inched, pulled, and squirmed their way to the summit, oblivious to the great heights and dizzying drop-offs of their objective.

Whey they finally stood on the peak's narrow arête they located the cairn of their predecessors, marked by an alpenstock and a tattered American flag. Returning to base camp they met up with the other members of the party, spending one more night in their secluded campsite before returning to Cooke City.[15]

Clyde traveled to the Sawtooth Range of Idaho, where he made at least seven more climbs before returning to California. After resuming his responsibilities at Independence High School, Clyde continued to climb on his weekends throughout the fall and into winter, recording his forays on a weekly basis. Clyde did not miss a weekend of climbing from the end of August until the end of November, when he appears to have had a two-week hiatus. His last recorded event of the year came on December 13 of 1926, when he went "up crest to 12,000 feet from Glacier Lodge."[16]

Clyde made some notable first ascents in 1926 as well. He recorded two first ascents of Mt. Russell on the same day, June 24, 1926, both Class 3 climbs, requiring the use of hand- and footholds and often a roped belay; Clyde first climbed the east arête and descended and then achieved the summit a second time that day by climbing the north arête. As Hervey Voge writes in *A Climber's Guide to the High Sierra*, "This peak presents a formidable appearance from almost any direction, and was one of the last of the major Sierra peaks to be climbed."[17] That the same man climbed it twice in one day by two different routes was a notable accomplishment.

Touring Topics editor Phil Townsend Hanna suggested to Clyde that a suitable peak for a first ascent was El Gobernador, or the Great White Throne, in Utah's Zion National Park. Clyde responded that he had "looked at El Gobernador, but made no attempt to scale it....I do not care much for sandstone, sloping at a precarious angle. It is too likely to scrape a lot of meat off a fellow's bones. If I am going to fall I would prefer to fall straight down."[18]

By 1927 Clyde was gaining a reputation as a "prodigious climber of mountains," even among fellow mountaineers,[19] and he often climbed the same peak numerous times. When he was living in Northern California, he climbed Mt. Shasta ten times, and held a speed record for one particularly fast ascent. He also seemed to have a particular fondness for Mt. Whitney, the highest peak in the continental United States at 14,494 feet. He would climb the peak more than fifty times over the course of his life, and in 1927 alone it was his target three times, making a grand total (to that time) of nine climbs of the peak. In the summer of 1927, he also returned to pioneer the west arête of Mt. Russell, climbing the peak three times in two years and being the only person to achieve the summit during that period. Similarly, Clyde pioneered routes on Mt. Agassiz in 1925 and 1927 and made two first ascents of Table Mountain, on the Great Western Divide, in the summer of 1927—the first with a group of seven people, including a young Glen Dawson, on July 26. Three days later Norman returned alone to climb the south face.

Wilson relates the story of Clyde leading a group up Mt. Ritter. The day before he was to lead the climb, he disappeared from camp, only to reappear at the end of the day. When the party set out for the summit on the following morning, Clyde "took them rapidly and unerringly to the top." It was then that the party discovered that he had been performing a reconnaissance of the peak, climbing it alone the day before "for practice."[20]

There was always, and would always be, a bit of the teacher in Clyde, helping those who found themselves challenged by the experience. In the summer of 1927, after a winter of heavy snowfall, a group of boys known as the Trailfinders and their leader, Carl Sharsmith, were making a trans-Sierra trek over Army Pass and down to the San Joaquin Valley. They crossed Harrison Pass at the headwaters of the Kern River, bushwhacking in the best sense of the word, descending snowy slopes and pushing through thickets of willow en route to a camping site near East Lake. Sharsmith wrote many years later, "Across the canyon just to the north, I saw on a slope the ruddy glow of a campfire. I thought I'd go see. Sitting alone and oiling his boots the gentleman that introduced himself was Norman Clyde. We had a long chat. He was engaged in climbing the nearby peaks: Crag Ericson, Mt. Genevra, etc."[21] Nelson P. Nies was on that trip with Sharsmith. He recalled "coming down after dark, and it was good to see his [Clyde's] campfire in the distance, and to camp with him. I was 16 years old."[22] As the group approached his camp, near a clump of whitebark pines, Clyde told them to "come on in, boys. You'll need two campfires, one that's bright to cook by, and one that'll last to keep you warm."[23] The following day Clyde gave them directions for climbing Mt. Brewer. The group headed north while Clyde continued south. They didn't encounter him again on the trail that summer, but it was a memory that would stay with Sharsmith and his charges for the rest of their lives.

There remained hundreds of peaks for Clyde to climb after the 1927 season. He made one road trip that summer, back to the Sawtooth Range in Idaho, but the rest of his summer was confined to the Sierra. Following the resumption of school in early September, Clyde continued his weekend forays into the mountains, making October ascents of Mt. Whitney and Mt. Muir and, two weeks later, a climb of Bear Creek Spire. As fall lapsed into winter, he limited his activity to east of the crest, including Independence and Kearsarge Peaks.

Close Ups of Our High Sierra

Perhaps one of the most significant events of 1928 was the publication of Clyde's first articles in *Touring Topics*. From April to July the magazine featured his articles, which detailed his activities of the past several years, calling them "'Close Ups' of Our High Sierra: An Intimate Description of California's Noteworthy Mountain Peaks, From the Mountaineer's Perspective." Photographs that Clyde had taken accompanied the lengthy articles, and for the first time they depicted a part of the state that the general public had never before seen. The first article focused on 14,000-foot peaks, beginning with Mt. Whitney. Clyde acknowledged that the view of the mountain that most people have, looking up from Owens Valley, is underwhelming, "but it is from the seldom trodden vantage points that Mt. Whitney is most imposing. From Lone Pine Peak, Mts. Mallory and Irvine, LeConte and Langley to the east and south; from Mts. Russell, Barnard and others to the north. Mt. Whitney is spectacular to a degree that would surprise those who have seen it only from the usual viewpoints. The panorama beheld from Mt. Whitney is one of great extent and magnificence. To the north it extends along the axis of the range to the mountains of Yosemite; to the west it looks across the Kern Basin to the castellated Kaweahs and the jagged line of the Kern-Kaweah divide; to the south, over gradually lowering forest-clad mountains;

to the east and southeast, over a multitude of arid ranges and desert valleys."[24]

The narrative continues on in this fashion, describing the height of each peak, its accessibility, and the magnificent views to be had from its summit. Clyde describes the other 14,000-foot peaks, grouped by location: the Mt. Whitney group, Mt. Williamson, and the Palisades. He saves his greatest praise for North Palisade, calling it "one of the most striking peaks in the Sierra Nevada. Probably the view from its summit equals in scope and magnificence that obtained from any peak in the range and without being unusually hazardous or difficult, it is sufficiently so to render it interesting to the most skilled mountaineer."[25] It's not surprising, then, that Clyde would choose to live below the Palisades at Glacier Lodge for twenty years as a winter caretaker, where he could easily view and access these rugged peaks.

The remaining three installments of "Close Ups" detail successively lower peaks: Part II covered those between 13,500 and 14,000 feet (May 1928); Part III, those between 13,000 and 13,500 feet (June 1928); and Part IV, those between 12,000 and 13,000 feet (July 1928). In each section, Clyde begins with the Great Western Divide and continues north along the range to the Yosemite region. Along the way, he discusses peaks on the Kings-Kern Divide, the Rae Lake basin, the Evolution Basin, the Minarets, Mts. Lyell, Conness, and Dana; Dunderberg, Matterhorn, and Tower Peaks; and the Clark Range.

Clyde's fondness for the southern Sierra is readily apparent. He preferred the high, lonely peaks and glacially carved basins to Yosemite's waterfalls and granite cliffs (not to mention its hotels, roads, and tourists). He wrote, "Although surpassed by the southern Sierra in loftiness and ruggedness of mountain scenery, the Yosemite region is superior to it in waterfalls and cascades, and, as it contains the Yosemite Valley in canyons also. As a whole, although not so epic in grandeur as the southern portion of the range, it is a charming and fascinating region with few equals anywhere in varied interests." And, Clyde might have added under his breath, "too damned many people!"

Until "'Close Ups' of Our High Sierra" was published, no one had written such a detailed travelogue of the mountainous high country of California's Sierra Nevada. While the Brewer party, Clarence King, and Dick Cotter had first explored the Sierra in the early 1860s and made their findings known through their journals, it was not until Clyde came along that one man climbed all of these peaks, often multiple times. Brewer, King, and others spent only a limited amount of time in the mountains, whereas by 1928 Clyde had already devoted almost half his life to mountaineering. That he could discuss with ease, and in great depth, dozens of mountains, covering thousands of square miles, proved to the mountaineering community and to the layman that he was the authority on mountaineering in the Sierra Nevada.

But Clyde wasn't one to rest on these laurels. On May 6, 1928, he climbed Temple Crag (12,999 ft.). Clyde believed that "it is doubtful whether there is a more beautiful and striking 'crag mountain' in the Sierra Nevada. Its northern and northeastern faces are sheer precipices varied by numbers of spiry, turret-like pinnacles, beautifully placed. The ascent is a thrilling, but not especially dangerous, rock climb, and has been accomplished several times. The view from its summit is circumscribed, but as the crag stands near the center of the Palisade amphitheater it affords, perhaps, the best view to be had of the great cirque walled in to the south by the magnificent Palisades, whose dark serrated forms rise above a series of glaciers that cling to their bases and send icy fingers far up the steep chutes that furrow their northern fronts."[26]

On subsequent weekends prior to the end of the school year he climbed Gould Peak, Mt. Gould, University Peak, Mts. Mallory and Irvine, and Mt. Whitney, again. As soon as school let out he climbed the North Palisade, then drove north to climb in the Minarets, where he made a first ascent of the peak that would later bear his name (Clyde Minaret, 12,281 ft.).[27]

The Sierra Club in the Canadian Rockies

The 1928 Sierra Club outing was a first in many ways for the organization, and for Clyde personally. It was the farthest the club had ranged in its twenty-seven-year history of outings, and it was the first large Sierra Club outing composed of climbers, hikers, and sightseers to visit a distant wilderness area where climbing wasn't the highest priority.[28] A specially arranged and equipped train was engaged for making the trip from Oakland to Jasper Park Lodge. En route the train stopped in Oregon and Washington to pick up fellow mountaineers from the Mazamas and Mountaineers clubs, respectively. When the group steamed out of Jasper Station, headed to Geikie Station, they were accompanied by two brothers, Hans and Heinie Fuhrer, who would serve as climbing guides for the remainder of the trip.[29]

Barbara Norris Bedayn was on the Sierra Club outing to Canada, a brand-new member who had been encouraged to go on the trip by her friend, Charlotte Mauk. Mrs. Bedayn recalled seeing on the train an "oldish" man sitting alone and looking sad. Taking the seat next to him, she struck up a conversation with the stranger, asking him if he had ever been to the mountains. He replied, "Well, I've seen a few." She also liked to ski, and asked him if he had ever tried it. He was warming up to her now, and was visibly in a better mood. He smiled and said, "Well, I've had the boards on." She left him smiling, and she felt good about the exchange.

The next morning Richard Leonard asked if she wanted to meet Norman Clyde. Knowing of his exploits, she said yes. Mrs. Bedayn says she "almost fell through the floor. I was the person who gave Norman Clyde advice on how to get along in the mountains."[30]

After the party detrained at Geikie Station, they made the long, sixteen-mile trek to their base camp at Moat Lake. From their campsite they could scan the wondrous view of the Canadian Rockies, including many peaks that the advanced climbers would ascend in the weeks to come: Redoubt, Drawbridge, Bastion, Turret, Geikie, and Barbican, all part of the formidable Rampart Range.

Meanwhile, a party of nine climbers, including Clyde, had left the train at Jasper Station to climb Mt. Edith Cavell. This would prove to be a good introduction to Canadian-style mountaineering for the group, as everything about the climb—from the long trudge through wearisome muskeg to the steep snow- and ice-covered slopes were new to the California climbers. As Bestor Robinson reported,

> We were confronted with a thousand feet of steep, crumbling knife-edge. To add to our contemplation of this scene, a cutting cross-wind was whipping through the saddle. Half-way up the knife-edge the harder quartzite gave way to a soft crumbly shale. The absence of safe handholds and footholds forced the abandonment of this route. Our Mazama friends, Don Woods and Ed Hughes, without hesitation swung out onto a sixty degree slope of ice and snow which terminated in a sheer drop onto the Ghost Glacier. We Sierrans, unaccustomed to snow, attempted

to scale the rock-slopes at the right, using ropes as a precaution; but finding this course impossible, we timidly followed our Mazamas onto the ice, sinking our ice-axes and crampons deep into cut steps. The Sierrans, who had laughed at the Mazamas on the ticklish rockwork, were now the recipients of well deserved humorous comments. So in this fashion we all got to the summit—Rusty [Marion] Montgomery, Norman Clyde, Don Woods, Ed Hughes, Oliver Kehrlein, Jr., John Olmsted, Bill Horsfall, Horace Breed.[31]

Following the descent and a night in camp, they made the long trek through a snow storm, across the Astoria River, and through flower-filled meadows to join their companions long after dark at their base camp in Tonquin Valley.[32] The mountaineers practiced on several peaks, attaining the summits of Bastion, Drawbridge, Surprise Point, Clitheroe, Caniche, Vista, and Glacis Ridge.[33] The next peak that felt the tramp of Sierran climbers was Geikie, the highest mountain in the Rampart Range at 10,854 feet. By this time they were well prepared and warmed up. It was not enough for this small but dedicated group of climbers to remain in camp and enjoy the views of the peaks, "wreathed in storm clouds or standing sharply silhouetted against the blue sky." As Clyde wrote so tellingly in his account of the ascent of Mt. Geikie, "Mountains are more than a spectacle. For there seems always to issue from their summits a challenge to scale them."[34] Clyde and eight others joined the Sierrans and Mazamas on this trip. The climb was challenging, and the group was divided into two, with Hans Fuhrer leading one rope and Clyde the other. Climbing Geikie was thought to be difficult, but the loose rock and insecure holds required an extra degree of caution on everyone's part. It wasn't just the holds but the changing weather that forced the group to redouble its efforts. Snow was flying when they reached the summit, where they stayed only a brief time before descending. As darkness enveloped them, some members of the party opted for a bivouac of a few hours before returning to base camp.

The next climb launched by the intrepid group was Mt. Robson, the highest mountain in the Canadian Rockies and known as "the Monarch." The formidable peak had first been climbed in 1907, although the summit was not reached until 1913. Conrad Kain, who led the first ascent, said that the climb was one of the most dangerous expeditions he had ever led, due to extreme weather, abundant snow and ice, and numerous rock avalanches.[35] The Sierrans were well aware of the hazards, as they had carefully studied the accounts of previous attempts published in the *Canadian Alpine Journal*. Prior to their climb, the summit had last been reached by four different expeditions in 1924, three of which were led by Kain and the fourth of which included six women, a first for Robson.

Three guides—Hans and Heinie Fuhrer and Joe Saladana—led the party of twelve climbers. The group left the Sierra Club camp near Dennison and Brittain's ranch in the valley of the Grand Fork on July 21. They were planning on a three-day excursion. The first night was spent at the upper end of Kinney Lake, and the following day the group made camp far above the timberline and just below the lower ice wall. The deep, loud booming of calving ice blocks punctuated the still, cold night air.

Breaking camp at 1:30 a.m., they began to climb just after 3:00 a.m. Each of the three guides led a group of three people; Norman served as the leader of a fourth group of three. At the summit of the Black Pyramid, the highest point of the southwest ridges, they were perplexed to find only icy obstacles in their way. Hans and Heinie consulted with great earnestness in their native tongue about what options were open to them. Much to the surprise of the group, Hans attacked with his axe a nearly vertical wall of ice that overhung a precipitously steep couloir, slowly chopping steps into the formidable mass. Heinie and Norman took turns belaying Hans, crouched as they were in a small indentation in the ice wall.

After an hour of chopping and climbing, Hans let out a shout, signaling to the group that he had safely made a ledge from which he could belay the other climbers. Heinie followed, and then Norman tried. Because he was stiff from his stint belaying Hans from his cramped niche, Clyde made several unsuccessful attempts to ascend the ice wall.[36] Something interesting happened next. Don Woods, a member of the Mazamas Club, tied his ice axe to his belt and, securing himself to the belay line, clambered up the forty-foot face in good time. The crux for Woods—and Clyde, who followed—was putting their faith in the rope and in their belayers. It was perhaps a seminal moment in the evolution of Clyde's climbing career, as he put his trust in both another climber and a new technique that would allow him to test the limits of his abilities. Rusty Montgomery followed, and because of the relative lateness (10:30 a.m.) and the distance that they had still to cover, the guides decided that they had reached the limit of people they could lead safely to the summit and back before nightfall. The others in the party cheered them on, offering encouragement and perhaps expressing their relief at not having to climb the two-hundred-foot ice wall. As for those at the top of the wall, their "happiness was made perfect by sardines—and cigarettes for Heinie."[37]

Several difficult pitches later, the group of five (Clyde, Woods, Montgomery, and the two Fuhrers) stood on the summit. After surveying the hundreds of square miles of peaks, glaciers, and lakes that surrounded them, they began their descent. It was 3:15 p.m., and it would take another four and a half hours to reach the top of the ice wall. The descent was "great fun" for all but Hans, who was bringing up the rear and nearly plunged into the couloir.

There were no other incidents as the party made its way down the steep ridges and icy slopes, arriving at camp well after midnight. After a restful sleep, the reunited group made their way through the Valley of the Thousand Falls to Berg Lake, Robson Pass, and on to the Sierra Club base camp at Lake Adolphus.

Across the Valley of a Thousand Falls stands Mt. Whitehorn, the last peak to be climbed on the 1928 outing. By this time the climbers had dwindled to six: Marion Montgomery, John Olmsted, Lowell Whittemore, Norman Clyde, and Hans and Heinie Fuhrer. It was now August 1, and the weather was turning sour; the constant rain had dampened their spirits but not enough to deter them from their climb. They had endured bone-chilling fog and snow at the higher elevations but pushed on, reaching the summit at 2:00 p.m. Because the top of Whitehorn was covered in snow, they built a new summit cairn, recorded their names on a piece of paper, stuffed the paper in a can, and stashed the can in the cairn. Because of the late hour they wasted no time in their descent.[38]

The group chose a different route in order to proceed directly to Kinney Lake and thereby save time. However, steep cliffs, ice walls, and a waterfall hindered their progress, and the group was forced to bivouac in a small patch of scrub oak. They spent a long, cold night huddled by their small fire, without benefit of adequate food or blankets. The following morning was equally frustrating, as one long descent ended abruptly at the top of a steep cliff, forcing them to retrace their steps all the way back to the site of their bivouac. Changing strategies and direction, the party now headed west, following a lateral moraine. Tired and very hungry, the group ended up returning by a new route, eventually reaching Dennison and Brittain's ranch, where they joined the rest of their compatriots for supper.

Back at camp on the shores of Lake Adolphus, two campfires flickered on the faces of the weary mountaineers. The photographer and violinist Cedric Wright played his music for the assemblage. "The thoughts of many of the party turned naturally on this occasion to the kindly sympathetic leader who has planned and led all of the Sierra Club's twenty-seven outings and to what he has done for the club, and through it for all lovers of the great outdoors." A heartfelt tribute to William E. Colby followed: "As he [Colby] stood in the glow of that camp-fire on the shore of Lake Adolphus, one after another of the party spontaneously voiced appreciation of the service he has rendered. Those sentiments were further expressed at the next and last camp-fire when, the party once more united, farewells were said, and the good fellowship was voiced in songs lasting far into the night."[39]

The following day Hans and Heinie returned to their home in Jasper, Alberta, and the members of the Mountaineers, Mazamas, and Sierra Club boarded the train for the long ride home. For Clyde, who returned to Owens Valley and his principalship at Independence High School, it would be his only climbing experience in Canada. Perhaps in addition to learning something about rope work and belaying from the Fuhrer brothers, he made a mental note of their life in the mountains, working as guides in the European tradition in the mountains of western North America. It would soon be a course that Clyde himself would embark upon.

High-Low

Clyde was aware of the importance of promoting not only the mountains but his own exploits as a way to further his career as a mountain guide. On one occasion, he decided that it would be "a novel and worthwhile feat to attempt a journey from the summit of Mt. Whitney to Death Valley between sunrise and sunset." This ambitious jaunt took place in September 1930.

Clyde ascended to the Whitney summit on September 6, via the new "horse trail." He made the climb of nearly 8,000 vertical feet in less than six hours. Clyde called the ascent "a pleasant but an expeditious one....It had, however, not been an over-strenuous one as I had swung along at a steady, rhythmic pace which never obliged me to stop for breath. This was due partly also to the grade of the new trail, which, except for occasional short pitches, rarely exceeds 15 per cent." Clyde camped on the summit, "in a small space of disintegrated granite behind the Smithsonian cabin," and in the morning was greeted by a brisk, cold wind. He hurried onto the trail, arriving at the trailhead in three and a half hours.

Jumping into a waiting vehicle, piloted by Carl Bruno of Lone Pine, the pair headed out for Death Valley, where the temperature at Stovepipe Wells was 116 degrees in the shade. Clyde "longed for the frigid night winds of the summit of Mt. Whitney. But the record objective of the trip had been achieved, since we had motored from Lone Pine in an actual driving time of less than three hours." The total time elapsed from the top of Mt. Whitney to Death Valley was about seven hours. Clyde concluded his essay by writing, "Toward evening we turned our faces westward in the direction of the Sierra Nevada. As the afternoon advanced the coloring of the mountains appeared to become richer and deeper; their perspective to lengthen and deepen. It had indeed been a day of varied experience. Starting at sunrise from the arctic-alpine summit of Mt. Whitney, within a few hours we were sweltering in Death Valley, the lowest and hottest valley."[40] Phil Townsend Hanna, editor of *Touring Topics,* included a sidebar titled "TRY THIS for an adventure!" What followed: "This is the latest accomplishment of the pedestrian-motorist Norman Clyde, a frequent contributor to these pages. Californians were interested to read briefly in the daily press in September of Mr. Clyde's curious adventure. In this article, prepared expressly for *Touring Topics,* he gives the details in that simple and unaffected style which has [been] featured [in] his many other articles on mountaineering."[41]

The East Face of Mt. Whitney

An important event in Sierra Nevada mountaineering history was the first ascent of the east face of Mt. Whitney, in 1931. The climb of the east face and east buttress was accomplished by the use of the belay, a European technique introduced to the Sierra in 1931 by Robert L. M.

Underhill. Francis Farquhar, vice president of the Sierra Club, had invited Underhill to California to climb with the Sierra Club. Underhill, a Harvard professor and renowned climber in the United States and in Europe, brought the techniques of belaying with ropes and pitons to the Sierra Nevada, where previously climbers had relied on their hands and feet, and on the occasional rope to haul or secure one another, sometimes with disastrous consequences.[42] Farquhar, who organized the climbing party that would make the attempt on the previously considered unscalable east face of Whitney, chose, along with Underhill and Clyde, two young men who would make climbing history of their own: Glen Dawson of Los Angeles and Jules Eichorn of San Francisco. Eichorn and Dawson had just completed a Sierra Club training camp with Underhill in the Ritter Range, where the professor was teaching Sierrans about the use of ropes in technical climbing. Underhill was impressed with their skills and maturity and did not hesitate to invite them to join the veterans on Whitney's east face.

Eichorn wrote years later of his strong desire to meet Clyde, who by then was a legendary figure in climbing circles. Eichorn wrote, "I first saw Clyde standing in the sun in front of Glacier Lodge, a jut-jawed, blue eyed, ruddy complexioned, animated block of granite....The impression which immediate[ly] was impressed on my mind was that here was a man who had made up his mind what he had to do and would never swerve from his objective. But I asked myself, 'how could a man with a [stocky] build like Norman's be such a good mountain climber?' I was soon to find out."[43]

As a warm-up climb, the party made a first ascent of an unnamed peak in the Palisades on August 13. Clyde, Underhill, Farquhar, Dawson, Eichorn, Bestor Robinson, and Lewis Clark were all in the party. Jules Eichorn recalled many years later in an unattributed interview,

We approached this peak that didn't have any name. We were not interested in naming or anything like that, we were just interested in climbing. We went to the Palisade glacier, got into one of the chutes on the east side that ran up more or less to the peak. We got to the base of the peak, and it was very precipitous, to say the least. It was sharp on all sides, like an obelisk. I guess it was Glenn who made the first ascent, because he was lighter and I gave him a shoulder stand. He stepped first on my knee, then on my shoulder. Pretty soon he could reach up, he found little nubbly handholds, they got us to the top. After we got a few people on the top, we as a group realized that this could become serious, although it didn't seem that important at the time we first saw the clouds to the south. In a very short time, I mean five to ten minutes, this storm had expanded to the point where we were involved in it. It was a thunderhead type storm. Everybody got off the peak and started getting lower. I was the last one off the peak and about 15 or 18 feet off its base and just below when the first bolt of lightning struck the summit with an unbelievably thunderous crash. It literally exploded in our faces. It was deafening and very upsetting because there's not much place to go on top of a 14,000 foot crest and it's steep going all the way.

Then there was another bolt. It must have been close because of the same noise. On the west side and down 30-40 feet we found a little curve that afforded protection. We all huddled under this thing. We realized we were in a bad spot, things getting wet, we had tennis shoes, the only one with decent shoes was Norman. He always climbed with hob nailed boots. Norman Clyde was leading us. He knew a better way to get off and into a chute that wasn't so steep. We were soaking wet, miserable, cold. We were able to cross the bergschrund, which is also difficult, but at that point we didn't know how steep it would be getting down the chute. But we had to get into it and get out of it, and get out to the glacier so we could walk home. I think we got back to our camp around 12:00 o'clock midnight. I think we were delighted with the fact that we had had a marvelous experience that we would not wish to have happen again, at least in the same way.[44]

The experience solidified Clyde's reputation as not only a great mountaineer but also a skillful leader who could take charge under the most difficult of circumstances. The summit became known as Thunderbolt Peak, to commemorate a stormy and dangerous first ascent.

The experience on Thunderbolt did not deter most of the climbers. (Robinson and Clark opted out.) The group approached Whitney Portal on the morning of August 15, 1931. They used mules to transport their packs for the first four miles up the trail, until they reached 9,000 feet and the north fork of Lone Pine Creek. There they shouldered their packs and, leaving the trail, began to trudge to the base of the massive peak. They made camp in a secluded meadow at the 10,000-foot mark, where they were greeted the following morning by a "rosy-fingered" dawn. Eichorn would later recall the "mild trip prior to the first ascent of the east face of Mt. Whitney, mild because of Norman's uncanny ability to find the easiest route from Whitney Portal to East Face Lake. Not only did all the ledges connect but on them were patches of ripe, juicy currants, just as Norman predicted."[45]

The following morning the party continued to make its way toward the base of the monolith. There they stashed any unnecessary gear, taking only two one-hundred-foot lengths of rope and a handful of pitons.[46] With that, the four men ascended into climbing history.

They divided themselves into two groups: Underhill and Dawson on one rope, Eichorn and Clyde on the other. For the latter two it was to be a pairing that would last throughout Clyde's life.

The climb was the most challenging of any Clyde had attempted in the Sierra, involving as it did numerous Class 4 and Class 5 pitches, which were new to Clyde's experience in the Sierra.[47] While attempting the Tower Traverse, Clyde swung out over the wall, dislodging a rock that he had chosen for a foothold. Fortunately, he was using his three-point system—that is, always having at least two feet and one hand (or two hands and one foot) on secure holds at all times. Nevertheless, it took Clyde a little while to regain his composure. The lead rope of Underhill and Dawson traversed the buttress and Clyde and Eichorn followed a short time later.

After negotiating what came to be known as the "Fresh Air Traverse" because of its extreme exposure, the climbers "corkscrewed" or shimmied up a chimney, and made their way to the summit. There, Francis Farquhar was waiting to greet them. He had been with the party as they approached the face but had become ill and was therefore unable to accompany them. Instead, he had gone up the Mountaineer's Route to the summit, where he'd met with a group of Boy Scouts. He asked if they had seen anyone clamber up from the east face. They replied that it was impossible. At that very moment, Jules Eichorn's head "popped over the top and refuted the boys' statement."[48]

At the top, Farquhar took a photo of the four mountaineers who, despite their stoic countenances, were elated by their successful first ascent of Mt. Whitney's eastern face. After savoring the summit for more than an hour, the group broke up, with Dawson, Eichorn, and Farquhar heading south to climb Mt. Muir, while Underhill and Clyde went north to take a different route down. Clyde concludes his *Touring Topics* article on the trip with the following:

After an evening spent in consuming enormous quantities of food and lounging about a campfire, we retired to our sleeping bags under nearby foxtail pines solemnly silent beneath a sky spangled with innumerable stars overarching the mountains that loomed darkly around the basin. On the following morning we made our packs and proceeded down the canyon, pleased at having added another outstanding climb to the many already discovered in the Sierra Nevada."[49]

Clyde and Eichorn continued their friendship for many years after the climb. The two men liked one another and understood one another, respecting each other's lifestyles and admiring the other's accomplishments. Together they made many first ascents.

Following his successful ascent of Mt. Whitney's east face, Clyde continued to climb throughout the summer season and into the fall of 1931. He headed back to the Palisades, climbing the Middle Palisade before heading up the south fork of Bishop's Creek to ascend Mt. Thompson on September 7.[50] Clyde had made the first ascent of the northwest face earlier in the year, but on this occasion chose to return and re-climb the peak from the north side, the first time it had been scaled from the headwaters of the creek's south fork. His account of the climb, while otherwise unremarkable, shows the careful and methodical style with which Clyde approached his climbing. With his binoculars he scanned the 1,500-foot-high sheer walls that rose to the flattopped summit, examining the fissures and chasms that occasionally cut the rock wall's face.

Choosing a possible route, he began to work his way toward the base of the climb. More than once he met with a precipitous ledge or a boulder-clogged couloir that blocked his way. Retracing his steps, he would jam and wriggle his way up a chimney, edge along a narrow ledge, and hoist himself over knobby rock walls to the next vantage point. When he finally reached the sloping tabletop summit, he proceeded westward to climb the highest pinnacles on the mesa's edge. On top of the highest point he found a cairn containing a glass jar with the names of a half dozen of his predecessors, dating back as far as the first recorded ascent, in 1909. After enjoying his lunch and the view, Clyde made his way down the northeastern face, accompanied by a number of rosy finches that flitted in front of him. At one point, lowering his rucksack and ice axe, the axe came loose and clattered down a narrow chimney and over the cliff face. Rather that rappel down the rocky face, he carefully climbed down and retrieved his now-battered ice axe from the foot of the cliffs.[51]

In the small range of peaks called the Inconsolables, Clyde climbed Cloudripper before returning to the Evolution Basin to ascend Mt. Agassiz. Heading north, Clyde made his way up some Class 2 peaks, including Crystal Crag and Mt. Tom. Clyde called Mt. Tom "a beautifully symmetrical mountain when viewed from the summit of Mt. Humphreys, the South Fork of Bishop Creek, Owens Valley or from the summit of Bear Creek Spire and other peaks to the northwest. Its richness of coloring, chiefly soft reds and browns, is very pleasing to the eye."[52] From Mt. Tom, Clyde went on to record a first ascent of the northeast face of Bear Creek Spire on October 6. Bear Creek Spire was one of Clyde's favorite peaks, notable for its spring skiing and numerous unexplored routes.[53] Clyde wrote, "It is an unusually impressive mountain of the Matterhorn type. On all sides, except the west, it drops away in almost vertical walls hundreds of feet in height. The summit itself is a single monolith only a few feet in diameter from which these jagged aretes radiate in true Matterhorn fashion.... This is in fact one of the most aerial perches of the higher summits of the Sierra."[54] Clyde returned the following spring, and on May 27, 1932, made the first ascent of the northeast arête.[55] His detailed accounts of climbs have proven useful to other climbers who have followed his lead; they also serve as insight into his method of route finding. Careful, unhurried, and with a trained eye for reading rock faces, he relied not only on his equipment but on his strength and agility to propel him up vertical walls and over knife-edge arêtes without any apparent heart palpitations.

CHAPTER 5

Desolate Grandeur: Rambles through Southern California

In addition to his High Sierra treks, Clyde spent portions of several winters in the mountains of Southern California. During the time he lived in Pasadena and attended USC he had several friends who were members of the Southern California chapter of the Sierra Club; one of his first Club forays was a climbing trip to Mt. San Jacinto in July 1917. Through the mid-1930s, Clyde also found favor as a lecturer at several Southern California locations; billed as a "noted mountaineer and writer," he gave talks at Switzer's Camp in the Angeles National Forest, and to the Trailfinders, a boys' outdoor organization in Los Angeles.[1]

His first extended excursion in the San Gabriels was in the late 1920s, perhaps 1929 or '30. He may have been retreating from his debacle at Independence High, seeking out the familiarity of the Southland; it would have been a time to reconnoiter, to assess his life and the new directions that it would take. Without a full-time job to report to, no dependents, and no permanent place to live, he may have felt somewhat at loose ends. The comfort and familiarity of the mountains offered him the solace he needed. He had not yet taken up snow skiing, so his ability to fully enjoy the Sierra Nevada in winter would not yet come for a few years, hence his long excursion to the milder but still wild mountains of Los Angeles County.

If one discounts the base elevation of the range, the San Gabriels are higher in elevation than the Rocky Mountains. The range is blanketed in snow during the winter, and subject to the sun's intense summer rays. The steep stream-cut canyons were quite different from the glacially carved canyons and cirques that Clyde had grown

45

accustomed to in the Sierra, but he nonetheless had an appreciation for the mountains of Southern California.[2]

On that first trip Clyde made a solo journey along the backbone of the San Gabriel range, beginning in Pacoima Canyon at the eastern edge of the San Fernando Valley. He observed the various birds that he encountered along the way, and noted how the vegetation changed as he climbed higher. Clyde wrote, "Lack of water on the first trip and heat on the subsequent one caused the canyon to appear inordinately long. A sleeping bag together with a week of provisions and various accessories, many of which a 'go light' knapsacker would have left behind, did not help matters greatly, neither did the fact that I was fresh from the snows of the High Sierra. While I patiently trudged along the trail around bend after bend of the winding canyon, perspiration flowed profusely down my face, forming an almost continuous stream down my nose, inducing me all too frequently to seek the grateful shade of live oak or water maple."

Clyde's trek took him along ridge tops and over pine- and chaparral-covered saddles. From time to time he was forced to walk along roads to reach the next trailhead. Because he was staying at high elevations, following the ridgelines from west to east and not dropping down into the canyons, water continued to be a most precious commodity. Toward one day's end he followed a sign for "Fountain Head Springs," which he followed to find another sign but no spring. "I seized my ice axe and started to dig vigorously at the damp spot. I was soon rewarded with seeing water ooze from the sides of the hole. When this was about two and a half feet deep I ceased digging and waited for the water to collect. There was presently about a bucket full of fluid which, although it contained a rather liberal amount of disintegrated feldspar in suspension, was used for tea and soup." The next morning Clyde took his leave of "Dig-Hard Springs" and continued down the trail.

Clyde resumed his trek despite poor trails, inadequate signage, and roads where he had not anticipated them. He made frequent wrong turns and sometimes followed routes for several miles before being forced to retrace his steps. From his account, he seems to have taken it all in stride, as he enjoyed the forests of big cone spruce, coulter pine, and incense cedar, as well as the creeks lined with alders, sycamores, and oaks. Once he was back on the trail Clyde continued for the summit of Mt. Williamson, named for the Army engineer who surveyed the San Gabriels for the Pacific Railroad Survey in 1853.

From the summit Clyde descended southward in search of Little Jimmy Spring, named for Hearst newspaper cartoonist Jimmy Swinnerton. He located a cache of food left there to relieve Clyde of "the necessity of descending some miles from the crest in order to procure them." He had some trouble locating Little Jimmy Spring, until he discovered a note left by a Mr. Turrill. "Thither I hastened, finding the [cache] intact and an excellent spring on a steep slope covered in tall pines and firs."

That night a rainstorm swept in and soaked the intrepid mountaineer. It continued all the next day and night, forcing Clyde to head for shelter at a lower elevation. At Crystal Lake, on the north fork of the San Gabriel River, he came across a construction crew working on a Los Angeles County recreation area. The county had leased 1,360 acres from the Forest Service in 1928 with the intent of building a campground, picnic areas, a marina, and a ranger station at the only natural lake in the San Gabriels. Prior to its development, Crystal Lake was a seldom-visited scenic wonder in the rugged mountains; the construction of a paved road to the camp had ended its sylvan isolation. Clyde walked into the camp and "although not accustomed to accommodat[ing] mountain vagrants, they offered to feed and house me until the weather should again become settled."

After several days and eight inches of rain, Clyde was once again ready to resume his mountain journey. He probably wiled away the time by reading, sleeping, and penning the beginnings of his article from which this account is taken. The vagaries of weather never seemed to bother him, as he accepted them as a natural part of life lived in the outdoors. As he trudged eastward he gradually gained elevation, encountering heavy snowdrifts and trees covered in ice. On one occasion a headache-sized chunk of ice fell from the top of a tree, grazing the brim of his hat.

Clyde caught his first glimpse of Mt. San Antonio, also know as Old Baldy, while climbing up North Mt. Baldy, the second highest peak in the range. Mt. Baden-Powell, as North Mt. Baldy is now known, is the site of a stand of "limber pine," the oldest living trees in Southern California. Making camp on a snowy patch of ground, he laid out his sleeping bag on a heap of green boughs he had cut for his bed. "The evening 'chores' done, I spent some time walking southwestward downward along the ridge and back to the summit [of North Mt. Baldy]. Its snow-covered summit glowing in the bright moonlight, Mt. San Antonio rose majestically across a deep, shadowy gorge. A billowing moonlit sea of fog covered the plain to the south-west; a smoke-like haze the desert to the north. Scattered lodgepole pines stood motionless in the cold, still atmosphere." Clyde was in his element.

He continued his trek eastward, marveling at the views of the steep, stream-cut mountains, the valleys, and the deserts. After a brief respite alongside a stream canopied by alders and maples he headed straight for the highest peak in the San Gabriel Range—Mt. San Antonio. From its 10,064-foot elevation, hikers can see as far as the southern High Sierra and San Clemente Island. Clyde trudged his way to the top, over deep snowdrifts, and made the summit after sundown. He found a snow-free patch of ground in the lee of some windshorn lodgepole pines and made his camp for the night, barely one hundred yards from the summit. The location gave him the opportunity to enjoy the view of the nearby San Bernardino Mountains bathed in moonlight.

The following day, Clyde descended Old Baldy and climbed Tele-graph Peak before wandering into Kelly's Camp on the northwest slope of Ontario Peak. At 8,300 feet in elevation the rustic resort was popular with mountain travelers such as Clyde, but it would never be a commercial success due to its distance from roads. Upon see-ing the rugged log cabins scattered among the pines and firs, Clyde was reminded of similar scenes in his beloved Sierra Nevada. Clyde climbed Ontario and Cucamonga Peaks before descending to the Cajon Pass, where he enjoyed a two-day rest before climbing in the San Bernardino range.

Lake Arrowhead was his first destination: "a sheet of blue water surrounded by hills with gentle lines and clothed with pine and oak, it reminds one of the lakes of Wisconsin or Minnesota." From there he struck out for Big Bear Lake. As he was exploring a shortcut to the water, his attention was drawn to a large rattlesnake near the trail. Using his ice axe, Clyde extracted the recalcitrant rattler from its hid-ing place. The now agitated snake assumed a defensive stance; Clyde took several photos of the viper before killing it. His attitude toward "varmints" was not uncommon for the time, and his actions, although viewed today as unnecessary, would have been considered appropriate and even laudable.

Clyde walked the nine miles along the south shore of Big Bear Lake to Pine Knot, where he had mailed himself a cache of food. He then proceeded south to climb Anderson Peak and San Bernardino

Above: The Clyde family, circa 1892. The boys in the back row are (left to right) Norman, John, and Arthur. They are standing behind their father, Charles, and mother, Sarah Isabelle. The girls are (left to right) Clara, Mabel, and Marion. Eva, Sarah, and Grace were to follow. Of the nine children born to Charles and Sarah Isabelle Clyde, seven reached adulthood and all of them graduated from college. Courtesy of Vida Brown.

Left: Norman Clyde enjoyed many outdoor activities, including a brisk game of tennis. Courtesy of Vida Brown.

Right: A pensive Norman Clyde keeping his gravely ill wife company at the La Vina Sanitarium in Altadena, California. Courtesy of Jules and Shirley Eichorn.

Left: Winifred Bolster Clyde reclining on the verandah of the La Vina Sanitarium in Altadena, California. Courtesy of Jules and Shirley Eichorn.

Norman Clyde, circa 1920. Note the gun holster partially hidden by his shoulder bag. Courtesy of the Eastern California Museum, Independence, California.

Mt. Whitney (14,494') is the highest peak in the continental United States. Norman Clyde ascended the mountain at least fifty times during his life, and was with the party that made the first ascent of the east face. Photo by Norman Clyde, courtesy of the Eastern California Museum, Independence, California.

In the foreground: Glen Dawson, Robert Underhill, Jules Eichorn, and Norman Clyde on top of Mt. Whitney following their successful first ascent of the east face, in 1931. Courtesy of Jules and Shirley Eichorn.

Jules Eichorn on the Milkbottle, the summit block of Starlight Peak in the Palisades. Eichorn and Clyde were friends for more than forty years. A high point for them both was their first ascent of Thunderbolt Peak, also in the Palisades, on the same outing this picture was taken, in August 1931. Photo by Norman Clyde, courtesy of the Eastern California Museum, Independence, California.

Above: The Minarets and Ediza Lake. Clyde Minaret is the highest peak on the left. Eichorn Minaret is to the right of Clyde, and Michael Minaret is to the left. This is the location of the dramatic search for Walter A. Starr, Jr., in August 1933. Courtesy of the Eastern California Museum, Independence, California.

Right: Norman Clyde with his trusty campaign hat, ice axe, and tricouni nailed boots. Courtesy of Jules and Shirley Eichorn.

Glacier Lodge in Big Pine Canyon, below the Palisades crest. Middle Palisade is visible at the top center. Clyde spent more than two decades as the winter caretaker of Glacier Lodge, and upwards of fifty years in the shadow of these peaks, one of which bears his name. Courtesy of the Eastern California Museum, Independence, California.

"The pack that walks like a man." Courtesy of The Bancroft Library, University of California, Berkeley, BANC PIC 1954.008 Box 2a.

Peak, resting for two days before ascending Mt. San Gorgonio. His campsite, 2,500 feet below San Gorgonio's summit, "had a certain fascination. Situated in a pocket, as it were, and shaded by tamarack [lodgepole] and limber pines, it possessed an atmosphere rather desolate yet somewhat alluring." His views from the summit the following day included Olancha Peak in the southern Sierra, Telescope Peak in the Panamints, and Mt. San Jacinto, his next objective, "standing out clear, to the minutest detail, in the sunshine of late afternoon."

The sunshine didn't last for long. On his approach to San Jacinto's summit he was caught in a drenching rainstorm. During his forced bivouac at 5,500 feet, Clyde spent his time cooking dinner and trying, somewhat unsuccessfully, to stay dry. He also busied himself with chopping firewood and observing the many species of birds that inhabited the area.

Clyde picked his way to the top of the boulder-strewn mountain, camping just below its summit. He arose early to be on top for the sunrise, and his description mirrored the stark but beautiful scene before him: "The Colorado Desert, more than 10,000 feet below, was a dismal ashen hue, while the gray-brown mountains beyond it were clothed in haze of a similar tone. In the dimness of the dawn the vast panorama had an aspect of impressive but desolate grandeur."

His last summit was that of Tahquitz Mountain, south of Mt. San Jacinto, after which he descended to Tahquitz Lodge, where he spent several days relaxing and exploring the numerous trails on horseback. Clyde returned to Los Angeles by automobile, thereby ending his six-week sojourn through Southern California's considerable wilderness. He had journeyed, on foot, more than one hundred and fifty miles, climbed several peaks, and gained and lost tens of thousands of feet in elevation. The trip resulted in a lengthy article in the April 1932 issue of *Touring Topics*, thereby cementing Clyde's reputation not just as a mountaineer but also as a mountain *man*.

El Picacho del Diablo

As we have seen, Clyde did not limit himself to the Sierra Nevada but ranged far and wide for wilderness experiences. His next big adventure would take him into Baja California to climb the highest peak in the region, El Picacho del Diablo. Standing high above the Sierra de San Pedro Martir Mountains of Baja California Norte, El Picacho del Diablo ("the peak of the devil") is as challenging as any peak in the Sierra Nevada. It is a difficult and complicated climb by virtue of its inaccessibility, long approach, and the elusive nature of its twin summits. Also, despite its 10,154-foot-high peak, the mountain is situated in a hot, dry climate, conditions that challenge even the most intrepid climbers.[3]

Dr. Edmund Heller of Chicago first approached the rugged peak in 1902. Professor Heller was in Baja not for the purposes of peak bagging but specimen collecting. The peak was first ascended by surveyor Donald McLain in 1911, who climbed alone to the summit. After that, the peak remained untrod for the next twenty-one years, until a party of Sierra Club climbers organized by Bestor Robinson and Glen Dawson, and including Norman Clyde, Richard Jones, Walter Brem, and Nathan Clark, approached the peak in June of 1932. Another member of the party, James Linforth, chose to botanize in the region of the Meling Ranch rather than climb the peak. Robinson had scouted the area in 1930 and was the only one of the party to have seen the region prior to the group's arrival.

Following the long drive down Baja's rough dirt roads, the party finally arrived at the Meling Ranch. They arranged for their dunnage to be packed across the fifteen-mile approach, with an elevation gain of 5,000 feet in 90-degree heat. The Mexican packer who accompanied them to the approach was incredulous that the band would shoulder their packs to walk up a mountain—"Todos locos," he reportedly muttered as he made his way back down the trail. Clyde paid special interest to the landforms and vegetation, comparing the former to the mountains of Southern California, which he had recently trod.

A lack of water continued to plague the group, as their trek took them over many miles of rugged country without benefit of stream or watering hole. The occasional small pool in a narrow canyon bottom was cause for celebration and rest before pushing on, higher up the mountain. They eventually made their way up one 10,000-foot summit from which they could survey the higher peak. It was decided that the most direct route was along a narrow arête to the west face, and from there to the top. Skirting along the west face, the first peak was soon attained, but a higher one loomed in front of them. The climbers, by now hot and tired and still unsuccessful in their attempt to achieve the highest point, decided to bivouac. The lack of water and, by then, food began to gnaw at their confidence. Robinson's discovery of a watering hole decided the evening's camping spot. Clyde later wrote, "The bivouac was a wildly picturesque one. Juniper and pine clung to the surrounding cliffs which seemed almost to impend over us and which presently glowed white in the light of the rising moon."

Their bodies rested and their confidence restored, the group started early the next morning for the summit, now thousands of feet above them as a result of their dogged search for water the previous day. As they got closer they noticed that there were two peaks of almost equal height; the group decided to climb both of them and leave nothing to chance in the record books. After ascending the south pinnacle the group dropped down, skirted the western face, and made the higher north peak. The view from the top was "grandly impressive." To the east lay the Gulf of California, with the Mexican mainland beyond; the Pacific gleamed bright to the west; and the desert, 10,000 feet below the climbers, surrounded their mountaintop throne.

The next challenge was to return safely to the Meling Ranch. Carefully picking their way down, they again visited the watering hole that had sustained them the previous evening. Then onward they went, bivouacking once again by yet another water source, and comforted by a raging bonfire. The next day they hastened to the ranch, where their companion, James Linforth, was getting ready to declare his companions missing and to request an airplane search for the lost party. Fortunately, they caught up with him before the SOS went out. After two days without food, the famished climbers ate a hearty breakfast before returning to Los Angeles and Oakland, proud of their ascent of Baja California's highest peak.

Clyde returned to Baja in April 1937 with *Desert Magazine* editor Randall Henderson to climb the peak from the east (desert) side. They approached via the mouth of La Providencia Canyon, a route unknown to both of these experienced explorers. The eastern approach involved more technical climbing than the earlier ascent, and even involved some traverses of snowfields that hide in the deep shadows of the steep granite walls. The duo achieved both south and north summits before beginning the long descent to the San Felipe Valley and enduring a rough ride home.

CHAPTER 6

A Candidate for a Padded Cell: Climbing through the Great Depression, 1932–1941

Clyde continued to climb throughout the Sierra Nevada for the next ten years, pioneering new routes and climbing some of his old favorites many times over. He led several Sierra Club climbing excursions, showing the way to literally hundreds of men and women who desired to stand on some of the high peaks surrounding their backcountry camps.

Regarding his penchant for climbing the same peak many times over, Clyde told Francis Farquhar in 1925, "I sometimes think I climbed enough peaks this summer to render me a candidate for a padded cell—at least some people look at the matter in that way. However, I get a lot of enjoyment from this rather strenuous form of diversion."[1] He elaborated on his love of climbing in an article entitled "Mountaineering in the Sierra Nevada." He wrote:

The most strenuous, yet to some the most enjoyable form of activity available to the vacationist in the Sierra Nevada is that of mountain climbing....The pleasures of mountaineering in the Sierra are manifold. They are physical, aesthetic and scientific. There is the enjoyment of the exercise involved in climbing the easiest of the peaks; that, together with the skill and courage employed in conquering the more difficult of the mountains. There is also the pleasure derived from an appreciation of the beauty and sublimity of the mountains—of the beauty of limpid brooks, green meadows and alpine flowers; the sublimity of deep cirques, profound gorges, precipitous crags and lofty peaks. There is also the enjoyment obtained from the study and observation of plant and animal life and of the structure and formation of the rocks.[2]

All of these things were an integral part of Clyde's existence, and through his writings and guiding activities, he was able to share some of the wonder and appreciation of the vast, rugged region with others.

Phil Townsend Hanna, longtime editor of *Touring Topics*, reported that he had received a batch of photographs that Clyde had taken, for possible publication in the automobile club magazine. Hanna reported that "all were of Sierran peaks, and the laconic inscriptions were something like this: 'Mt. Goddard (13,350 feet). Climbed four times.' 'Mt. Haeckel (13,422 feet). Climbed five times.' 'Mt. Darwin (13,841 feet). Climbed seven times.' The total of ascents for each peak is not correct, I know, but they were just as imposing. The point is that this chap flits about the Sierra as nonchalantly as most of us walk about our own homes."[3]

Another flitter of the Sierra was the young David Brower. His father had introduced the future Sierra Club director to the mountains, and together with some friends from his Berkeley neighborhood he expanded his knowledge of the mountains and became a pioneer climber in his own right. In 1933 Brower set out on a seven-week backpacking trip with George Rockwood. As a novice climber, Brower made an attempt of the Thumb in the Palisade group. A loose rock almost spelled the end of his climbing career. Two days later, while relaxing at Glacier Lodge, he related the story of his near-fatal climb to Clyde, who offered the young man valuable advice regarding three-point suspension—that is, in difficult climbing situations, have three secure points or holds while searching for the next move or hold.[4] Thirty years later, Brower would recall another gem of advice from the venerable mountaineer: "The mountain will always be there tomorrow. Aim to be able to say the same of yourself."[5]

Clyde only reported suffering from one climbing mishap. He related the incident to Tom Miller in an interview that appeared in *Climbing Magazine* six months before Clyde's death, in 1972. The injury occurred in the Palisades group, where Clyde was descending after retrieving a pair of crampons left by some unknown party on an earlier climb.

I cut a few steps getting up, and coming back down there was one bad step I tried to cut out a little more. What had happened, it had thawed underneath. The next steps were all good solid ice, but this one broke. I went over about 75 feet of glare ice, and I'd lost my ice axe. I didn't have it attached to my wrist. As I started down I kept my feet ahead of me and actually got myself pretty well under control. But I realized that there was a crevasse below me. The crevasses along there had a high upper lip. The upper lip would be maybe 20, 25 feet above the lower one. Sometimes (this was in late summer) they'd be filled in with fallen cornices and sometimes they'd be open. I didn't know if that one was open or not. I couldn't stop myself entirely before reaching it, and if I couldn't stop entirely, I would need enough momentum to carry me over the crevasse and light on the other side. So I hit the upper lip, shot across, and lit on the other side. But one crampon struck a sloping place. I lit with my feet in the right position, but my right foot was twisted very badly and I sprained my ankle. The only bad sprain I ever had. I could hardly walk. There was a fellow there that took my rucksack and went up and got my ice axe, so I was able to get back to the upper lodge and make camp. I stayed there several days....I didn't try to walk. I went around on my hands and knees instead. I had wood cut so I could cook and so on without being able to walk. In time, the ankle healed perfectly."[6]

Clyde's previous meeting with Dave Brower must have had an impact on both men, for in 1934 the forty-nine-year-old denizen of the mountains joined the twenty-two-year-old and his companion, twenty-four-year-old Hervey Voge, while the two young men were on a ten-week backpacking and climbing trip through the Sierra. Brower and Voge had met the previous year in Humphreys Basin while Voge was traveling south and Brower and Rockwood, north. Voge encouraged Brower to join the Sierra Club, and the latter agreed to make the ten-week trek in order to conduct a survey of Sierra routes and mountaineering records. The intrepid climbers made thirty-two first ascents, leaving "improvised" summit registers on many of the peaks and checking the conditions of registers on twenty-seven other summits.[7]

Clyde joined the two men at their camp at Fifth Lake, below the Palisades, on the evening of June 14, 1934, and the next day they proceeded to climb Mt. Agassiz. Following "three-days of marching, loafing and fishing," the trio arrived at Devil's Crags, on the south fork of Rambaud Creek. Brower wrote, "For the next three days there followed our most interesting mountaineering. We climbed ten of the low Crags and explored nine of the chutes. We climbed both roped and ropeless, and roped down in several places. Norman spent long periods with his ice ax, cutting steps for the party. We basked in the sun and chilled in the wind. Hervey built enormous cairns, and we left little registers. Each night we returned to one of our happiest camps— on a meadow-shelf, shaded by hemlocks and pines, with colorful cliffs, and graced by a lakelet, flower-bordered with cassiope-bells and cyclamen."[8]

Clyde penned a note to Ed Ainsworth, a popular columnist for the *Los Angeles Times*, and Ainsworth included it in his July 6, 1934, column, "Along El Camino Real." Clyde wrote:

One of the most remarkable mountaineering feats ever accomplished in the United States was the scaling from June 23 to 26, inclusive, of ten of the twelve major pinnacles of the Devils Crags. These are a savagely rugged group, or rather, line of peaks, averaging some 12,000 feet in elevation on the middle fork of the Kings River in the southern Sierra Nevada. Nine of the ten scaled on this occasion were first ascents.

The climbing was often most spectacular. Steps were cut for hundreds of feet up steep snow filled chutes, narrow shelves were traversed and wall-like pitches were surmounted. The most spectacular features of the ascents was the numerous "rope downs" engaged in by the party. (In roping down, after looping a rope about a projecting rock, passing it through a rope sling attached to one, or threading it through a piton—a ring-headed iron spike—the mountaineer adjusts the doubled rope spirally about his body and then either walks backward down the cliff or launches into space.) In one instance during these climbs, about eighty feet of sheer drop-off was negotiated in this manner.[9]

After spending two weeks with Clyde, it was time for Brower and Voge to head north. "In his company we had learned much of safety and precaution, and of the use of the ice ax, both for mountaineering and for domestic purposes. We had gathered bitss of geological and botanical nomenclature, and we had heard stories and anecdotes about the Sierra, and about those who love it and those who live too close to appreciate its attributes. Moreover, we had become acquainted with Clyde's technique of establishing 'boulevards' up the precipitous sides of peaks, particularly in the Palisade Group."[10] Three weeks later they encountered Clyde again, this time leading a Sierra Club group in Matterhorn Canyon, in northern Yosemite. It would not be their only encounter, either in the Sierra or at Matterhorn.

The following summer would find Clyde on his own once again. He was not yet fifty years old, and his love of the mountains continued unabated. During the course of the next twelve years he would complete another thirty first ascents in the Sierra Nevada, bringing his grand total to more than one hundred and thirty.[11] One of the more significant ascents of this period was the east arête of Mt. Humphreys. At 13,986 feet, it is the highest peak in the range north of the Palisade group, and a powerful block of granite when viewed from as far away as the town of Bishop in Owens Valley. Although it had first been climbed from the west as early as 1904, the eastern approaches remained daunting. Clyde pioneered challenging routes both ascending and descending the mountain, and was "somewhat elated at having succeeded in attaining the summit of Mt. Humphreys by the formidable and hitherto untrodden east arête and in making the descent by a route for the large part also original."[12]

Winters likewise found Clyde enjoying the mountains. Clyde's cold weather comfort was a byproduct of his boyhood and youth in the forests of Pennsylvania and Canada. There, the long, harsh winters prepared him for the hardships associated with living in a cold climate. In California, the idea of living at or above 8,000 feet was (and still is) a novelty. During Clyde's time, when California was the land of sunshine and the place where Canadians and Midwesterners flocked in the winter to avoid the snow and cold, it was downright ludicrous. And yet, he took a certain joy and pride in his chosen place of residence. In an unpublished article entitled "Wintering in the Sierra Nevada," Clyde outlined the necessary requirements for living beyond the road's end.

In the article Clyde also elaborated on some of his winter encampments. Although he does not mention most of them by name, it is possible to figure out where he was staying according to his descriptions. The most famous, of course, was his stint as a caretaker at Glacier Lodge in Big Pine Canyon, where he spent upwards of twenty years. "Except for a space to the east, I was completely hemmed in by high mountains. During the shortest day of the year, only three hours elapsed from the time that the sun appeared above the top of one mountain until it disappeared behind that of another. Occasionally, even in midwinter, I climbed the surrounding mountains on snowshoes. From their summits magnificent views of snow-covered peaks were obtained—views of which summer visitors to the mountains have little conception."[13]

Clyde spent several winters in the Bishop Creek watershed, "sometimes in a cabin, and others in a tent." He spent one winter (year unknown) in Giant Forest in Sequoia National Park, during which the latter half of January saw fifteen feet of snowfall in an almost continuous series of storms, and he spent another harsh winter at Glacier Point in Yosemite National Park. "This, too, proved to be a year of extremely heavy snow. From the Christmas holidays, for upwards of six weeks, storm followed storm in rapid succession. On an average of once every ten days I snow-shoed down to the Valley, usually returning the following day....Views of Half Dome, obtained through shifting storm clouds, were indescribably grand....I spent much time snow-shoeing hither and thither through the magnificent forest of pine, fir, and incense cedar....Once every several days, I snow-shoed to the top of Sentinel Dome, about a thousand feet higher than Glacier Point. The panoramic views of the high Sierra, buried beneath a heavy mantle of snow, were worth traveling far to enjoy."[14]

Clyde had long traversed the winter landscape in search of solitude, stunning vistas, and challenging climbs, and he preferred snowshoes for "strictly utilitarian purposes. They are better for carrying heavy loads, for the loose, powdery snow following storms, for traveling through thick timber or brush, for pulling a toboggan or sled, and for general 'choring about.'" For a mountain man, Clyde came to skiing relatively late, but once he discovered the delight of the popular winter sport, he mastered it and made it his own. In the winter of 1928–29 Orland Bartholomew sought Clyde as a companion on a trip to ski the length of the John Muir Trail, but the legendary mountaineer was not yet comfortable enough with his skiing abilities to accompany the seasoned snow surveyor. Bartholomew went on, spending more than three months traveling alone from Lone Pine to Yosemite. Perhaps it was this remarkable accomplishment that spurred Clyde to hone his own skills on skis. Many years later Clyde wrote,

I shall not forget...a sudden blossoming out, as it were, in my own skiing. For several years I had been making constant but not very rapid progress. Wishing to make certain ski climbs in the

Sierra Nevada, but feeling that my degree of skill in manipulating skis was scarcely adequate for such ventures, I decided to give my ski technique—or lack of it—a thorough overhauling.

Among other things my Christiana—Christie for short—turn, my "S" turn—was a rather poor affair....I was eager to master it and decided that I might not call myself a skier until I had acquired a high speed Christie...

To remedy the matter I first consulted a circular of instructions, written by a famous ski coach[,] and then with a careful inspection[,] both of my movements and of the turns as seen in the snow, some of the latter were incipient but not complete Christianas. The fault soon discovered and remedied, almost before I realized what was happening, the rear ski was swinging around almost automatically and I was making good, occasionally perfect "Christies."

Within a few days I was looping down slopes with a steepness of gradient that I would not have attempted a month previously. Also the rate of speed at which I could travel with reasonable safety was greatly increased.

Although I had not become a crack skier I had almost overnight, as it were, become an excellent one, merely through a little time spent in careful study of my methods. With[in] several weeks my skiing had improved fully a hundred per cent, and my enjoyment of it increased at an equal ratio.[15]

The above passage is classic Clyde. As an autodidact he set out to analyze and improve upon his skiing performance through solitary study. Upon achieving a desired level of performance, he continued to practice until he could pronounce himself an "excellent" skier, which he, in fact, was.

By 1936 Clyde was considered a good enough skier to be counted on to deliver a written message from eminent field biologist Dr. Joseph Grinnell to Annie Montague Alexander, an intrepid naturalist and collector who was snowbound in the remote Saline Valley. In a return note to Grinnell, Alexander wrote,

You can imagine our thrill on coming back to camp near noon on Wednesday—we had been after wood we had split in the wash—to find a man sitting by our tent, back pack and skis by his side[,] who proved to be Norman Clyde, trapper commissioned

by [Ward] Russell to find us. It had taken him two days to come
and he had cut across to the Bunker Hill Mine Tuesday night,
thinking to find us there and had spent the night. The miners had
so many letters to send by him that he was late in reaching us.
He handed me your letter of January 14 and while Miss Kellogg
prepared lunch and Clyde waxed his skis I wrote a hasty note
to Russell enclosing money and asking him to hire a tractor and
bulldozer if possible to get us out. Clyde's pack weighed about
50 lbs. and included his sleeping bag, tools and provisions—an
extra supply of the latter in case of emergency, some of which he
turned over to us to lighten his load, as eight eggs, bacon, butter,
sugar and cookies—very acceptable! We then took him up the
road six miles [by car] and partly into the snow. We might have
gone farther but were afraid we might get stuck—an icy north
wind was blowing. Clyde hoped to reach a placer miner's cabin
in Marble Canyon by night and go on to Big Pine the next day,
and yesterday was the coldest we have had here, ten degrees at 8
o'clock in the morning. He thought the road might be cleared in
a week's time.[16]

When late April and early May rolled around and Clyde had to
vacate his winter quarters, he would head up Bishop Creek or Rock
Creek Canyon for a month or two of spring skiing. In the April 1938
Sierra Club Bulletin Clyde reported that for several winters past he
had done a "good deal" of climbing and skiing in the headwaters of
Bishop Creek. "The extensive area occupied by this amphitheater, the
abundance of northern and northeasterly exposure, together with a
number of long gentle slopes, render this region one of the most desir-
able for skiing to be found east of the crest of the southern portion
of the Sierra Nevada. As yet, however, I presume that I am the only
person who has traversed any considerable portion of this magnificent mountain amphitheater on skis."[17] Clyde would either use the
area around Parcher's Camp as a base of operation or establish a high
camp at Treasure Lakes at the western base of Hurd Peak, more than
10,000 feet in elevation. From there he would climb to the crest of the
Sierra and summit "a peak or two" before returning to his skis for the
run back to camp. He carried with him a short pair of skis, no more
than five or six feet in length. He explained that "although one cannot
travel so fast on a 'straightaway' with skis of such short length…the
facility with which stemming and Christiana turns can be made on

steep slopes is likely to surprise one who has used only the longer ones. With the short skis a fairly expert skier can link down chutes that only a very good skier could descend with longer ones. By using this equipment I have climbed most of the peaks about the headwaters of the South Fork..."[18]

Clyde reserved his highest praise for Rock Creek Canyon, east of Tom's Place, a gas station, general store, and lodge located on Highway 395 at the top of Sherwin Summit. When Doug Robinson asked Clyde about his favorite ski runs, Norman went right to Bear Creek Spire, at the headwaters of Rock Creek, which he called "one of the finest" peaks in the Sierra Nevada; "perhaps no single high mountain in the Sierra affords more opportunities for skiing, or perhaps rather ski-mountaineering, than does Bear Creek Spire."[19] Later Clyde would expand that praise to include all of Rock Creek Canyon, which he told Robinson had "the finest skiing on the east side of the Sierra."[20] He would continue to ski into early summer, when the snow's quality and quantity deteriorated and other interests, such as climbing, fishing, shooting, or just rambling, overtook him. Many years later, he asserted that "although I claim to be the world's worst skier, I have probably done more ski mountaineering in the Sierra than anyone else."[21]

Of course, those many months of isolation could take their toll on any human being, and Clyde was no exception. There were times when he did not see or speak to another person for months on end. On more than one occasion he temporarily lost his ability to speak as a result of his quiet, isolated existence. And, he carved patterns of daily life for himself that were out of step with his contemporaries; whereas many other climbing and mountaineering companions pursued more traditional pursuits in cities and towns throughout California and the West, staying in touch via telephone, committee work, or weekend get-togethers, Clyde was alone in his high mountain camps until the arrival of summer and another year of Sierra Club excursions.

Although Clyde was recognized as a premier climber, perhaps the best in the Sierra Nevada at the time, he suffered from a lack of social graces. Dorothy Pepper, recalling the Sierra Club trips, said:

> There were things about the Club that were really undemocratic in those days. In climbing, they never put a sign up on a tree saying that there was going to be a climb up Mt. Everest or Mt.

Whitney or whatever mountain it was. They got up their own party and decided whom they would ask. It would be about seven or eight people. It was very exclusive and if you weren't asked to go with that climbing group, you didn't horn in.

Norman Clyde suffered from this. He was a great climber, but he was very anti-social, and he was never invited on any of those climbs. Never. When the rest of them would go off, he would form his own little group. He might suddenly say on a Saturday morning, "Well, let's go off and climb." He would get two or three women like Alice, Julie, Dottie Baird and maybe Jay Oaks, and that was it. They would go climb some mountain, and then they would come back. The women were camping with me, and they would nearly always get back late at night and come into camp....One time he took some gal out on a trip for the day. There was a terrible storm and they got caught in the rain. They didn't come back. When he did come back in the morning with this gal, Young Tap, who was lots of fun, [he] said, 'well, Norman, we better get out the prayer book. We're going to have to make a shotgun wedding here." Norman was furious. He just turned seven shades and walked away. He would never play along with any of those things. He just had hard luck all the time.[22]

Clyde's interest in promoting the activities of women mountaineers is not well known but is made apparent through the many accounts of women who were on Sierra Club outings in the 1920s and '30s. Olivia Johnson remembered that Clyde

...instituted Grandmother Walks, and they were posted as Grandmother Walks. They would not be very hard; they would not include a great deal of rock climbing, but they would go to the lovely places that you saw around you and wished that you could reach. He had only one absolute rule: he would not take anybody on a Grandmother Walk who had not learned to rappel down a rock face....He was also very anxious that you learn to leap from boulder to boulder, without stopping to teeter and balance yourself, because having an instinctive balance meant that you could move fast over a boulder field. If you had to stop and touch it with your fingers and wobble back and forth, it took a great deal of time.

He was a very pleasant director; he was firm, and he would very smartly say no if you were doing something foolish, but he was very good at cutting steps in icy snow fields and directing people, remembering to direct people to start with the right foot, or whichever foot was proper. He added a very nice element for older people to the base camps, that I appreciated tremendously.[23]

Clyde was employed by the Sierra Club as a guide throughout the 1930s. People liked Clyde's pace, as he was a slow, steady, methodical climber, although not always easy to get along with.

Perhaps the most vivid event that stands out and marks another turning point in Clyde's life occurred in the summer of 1941. It was the last summer that many of the Sierra Club's members would enjoy climbing together before the war drew many of them into the ranks of the Armed Forces. Clyde was leading a group up Matterhorn Peak, on the northeastern boundary of Yosemite National Park.[24] There was one man in the party whom Clyde didn't care for, but he went with Clyde at the insistence of the Sierra Club climbing committee and against Clyde's wishes and better judgment. While the group was crossing a steep snowfield on a 45-degree slope, the unidentified man (described by the director of the Sierra Club's "High Trips," Richard Leonard, as "a little bit clumsy") fell and broke his pelvis and suffered a severe cut on his scalp that required seventy-six stitches. Harold Kirker, a member of the climbing party and an eyewitness to the accident, recalls, "Clyde acted very badly. I was in the party and actually asked him to set up a rope over a passage which would have prevented the accident."[25] Richard Leonard later recalled that someone quoted Clyde as saying, "The hell with him [the injured man]. Let's go on with the climb."[26]

Someone did, however, dash back to camp, retrieve a stretcher, and return to the bloody scene. The injured man was carried back to camp, where Dr. Dexter Richards of Berkeley spent most of the night sewing the man's scalp back on to his head. The injured climber then spent the next two days being carried down to Tuolumne Meadows, where he was loaded into a car and transported to the hospital in Yosemite Valley.[27] Clyde, who claimed not to have had an accident in twenty years of guiding for the Sierra Club, recalled the incident in an interview almost thirty years later in this way:

I was cutting elephant steps across a snowfield couloir. I thought anyone in the world could walk across there. I was going ahead when one of the girls let out a squawk and I looked around. That fellow that I didn't want to take along was cartwheeling down. He hit some rocks and injured himself.

The next day when I took a party up to see what had happened, a fellow from New York slipped on an ordinary snow slope and fractured his tibia. If he'd just have dug his elbows or heels in, he'd have stopped, or nearly stopped...[;] he wouldn't have been hurt.[28]

David Brower, who was on the High Trip but not with Clyde on the day of the accident, later confirmed that two other accidents occurred on the same snowfield on subsequent days. Brower recalled, "Norman was annoyed that the [first] victim had not properly used the footsteps Norman had punched into the snow for the party....For years and years Norman had 'barleysacked' people up difficult pitches when he had to, with bemused patience. On the Matterhorn climb he was impatient when sympathy was needed, and he had chosen too dangerous a course for the novices who followed him."[29] The only other person hurt by the incident high on Matterhorn Peak was Norman Clyde. Richard Leonard, David Brower, and other Sierra Club members present at the base camp held a board of inquiry and fired Clyde. He would never lead a Sierra Club High Trip again. The stinging rebuke stayed with him for years.

The official account of the trip, written by L. Bruce Meyer and published more than a year later in the *Sierra Club Bulletin* of August 1942, made no mention of the incident or of Clyde's firing. Clyde is credited with leading groups on "assaults" of Tower Peak, Snow Peak, and Matterhorn Peak.[30] Perhaps it was America's entry into the war five months later that momentarily eclipsed those events in northern Yosemite in late July of 1941; whatever the explanation, even if no one would write about what had happened, and few people would openly talk about it, many would nevertheless remember.

CHAPTER 7

Mountain Tragedies: Looking for the Lost and the Dead

Despite the incident on Matterhorn Peak that led to his dismissal from the Sierra Club's climbing programs, Clyde was better known for helping people who were in trouble in the backcountry, not hurting or neglecting them. For years he was one of the few skilled mountaineers in the Sierra who could be counted on to doggedly search for lost hikers, climbers, and fishermen long after others had given up. The search and rescue groups of the 1920s and '30s are a far cry from the professional crews that exist today. Now, when a climber or hiker is lost or injured in one of the many national parks, forests, or Bureau of Land Management regions, highly trained search and rescue (SAR) teams are dispatched to comb the area where the missing person was last seen. These efforts, depending on the length and complexity of the search, can involve dozens of persons, numerous pieces of high-tech equipment, and hundreds of thousands of dollars. By contrast, sixty and seventy years ago, when there were fewer wilderness travelers, searches for overdue hikers were usually conducted by volunteers, friends, and family members, or Sierra Club members experienced in climbing. The U.S. Forest Service and National Park Service had only limited resources and semiskilled personnel to retrieve the injured or the dead from remote areas of the Sierra Nevada. Rock climbing and mountaineering were still too new to the state, and government agencies too young, to mount extensive rescue operations. More times than not, if the missing party failed to materialize within several days, the search was abandoned.

Norman Clyde played a significant role in changing that attitude. His persistence and tenacity in searching for the dead and injured earned him a reputation as a rescuer that was almost as strong as his

notoriety as a climber. His ability to discern routes on craggy mountain faces helped him determine the whereabouts of a lost hiker or
climber, or the possible location of a body after a fall. He taught his
skills to several rangers who went on to perform their own daring
rescues and to develop search and rescue programs that have become
models for public agencies nationwide. Clyde attributed his success to
the "trait of indomitable perseverance," a self-aggrandizing statement
that, however true, appears with some regularity in the accounts of his
exploits.

Clyde's experience with rescue work began early in his career as a
mountaineer.[1] In 1927 Clyde was camped with several female Sierra
Club members at the base of the Kaweah group, having successfully
led his party to the top of Black Kaweah earlier that day. Another
Sierra Club climbing party was camped in the distance and Garth
Winslow, a Stanford University student in that other party, was eager
to make a solo ascent, despite an admonishment from Sierra Club
leader William Colby. Winslow arose at two o'clock in the morning and headed out for Black Kaweah on his own. When he failed to
return to his camp the following day, a search effort was organized by
Clyde. The young man's battered body was discovered on a side of the
mountain that had not been previously climbed. Winslow was carried
over several miles of trailless ground and talus before reaching a point
where his body could be lashed to a pack mule for the long ride out.[2]
Jules Eichorn, a youth of fifteen, was a member of the search party.
Many years later he said, "That's a messy job to be looking for someone, because you don't want to be the one to find the body. And yet
you have to, that's what you're supposed to be doing, that's why you're
searching. It's a hell of a way to spend your weekend."[3]

March 1929 found Clyde in Southern California. He was in Lytle
Canyon when he heard and responded to a group of boys crying out
for help. He found them with fourteen-year-old Paul Revert, who had
taken a two-thousand-foot tumble off Mt. Baldy. Clyde put the boy
on his back and trekked two miles to Glenn Ranch, where the boy was
transferred to nearby Rialto for treatment.[4]

The following year Clyde was pressed into service when eighteen-
year-old Howard Lamel of Los Angeles was climbing Mt. Whitney
with his brother and father and decided to try the east face on his
own. When his family members reached the summit and Howard did
not appear, a search ensued, entailing the efforts of more than one
hundred forest rangers and volunteers, as well as airplanes. It was not

until his father, Edward G. Lamel, requested the assistance of Clyde and Robert Evans that the young man's body was discovered in a crevice at 13,500 feet on the "all but inconquerable" east face.[5]

A similar incident occurred in Yosemite in 1932. A party of young climbers lacking in skill and proper equipment attempted to climb a steep chute on the trail from the valley floor to Glacier Point—a chute that Clyde and a Swiss guide had been up only days earlier. Clyde knew the dangers of this route and had taken precautions ascending and descending the icy slopes. Ice axes and nailed boots were the order of the day, but the two young men following in Clyde's ice axe–chopped steps had neither. The young men, Henry J. Blank and A. C. Manheim, tied themselves together using a length of 3/16-inch cotton clothesline and proceeded upward.

Blank lost his footing on the icy slope, tumbling down the icy chute and over the edge of a three-hundred-foot cliff. Still tied to the other end of the rope, Manheim was able to anchor himself to a large boulder, which not only prevented him from going over the edge but also kept his friend dangling above the abyss. Unable to pull his friend to safety, Manheim held on to the rope and yelled for Blank to try to climb the lifeline back to safety. The swaying of Blank's body on the other end of the rope, however, abraded the soft cotton rope against the sharp granite edge, and when the rope broke, Blank fell helplessly to his death. When Clyde investigated the incident later, he figured that the missing man—whose body had not yet been found—was either caught in a tree, wedged in a vertical chimney, or resting on a natural ledge of rock. After five hours of searching the icy face, Clyde finally discovered the corpse on a ledge. Blank was slowly brought back to the Valley floor, where his companion claimed the body.[6]

Although Clyde had an impressive record for recoveries, it would not go untarnished. There was the case of Norris Parent, a resident of Oakland who left Lundy Lake on the east side of the Sierra crest with the intent of hiking to Tuolumne Meadows in one day, a distance of some thirty miles. He never made it. The Forest Service and Park Service organized a search but without success. The only clue they found was a pair of sunglasses lying on a snow bridge over Lundy Creek. Clyde searched the area in August, returning again in October. He believed that Parent had stopped on a snow bridge to take a picture and the bridge had collapsed, throwing the young man into the swift snowmelt, where he drowned. Following the futile searches, Parent was ultimately declared dead by the authorities. Clyde noted that Parent was the only person lost in the mountains that he had searched for and was unable to find.[7]

One particular search made Clyde's reputation, and his account of the incident has become a classic in mountaineering literature. It involved a young attorney from San Francisco whose family were prominent citizens active not only in the Sierra Club but in other well-known Bay Area circles as well.

Walter A. "Pete" Starr, Jr., was born in Oakland, California, on May 29, 1903, the first son born to Walter and Carmen Moore Starr. He was raised in the East Bay and educated at Stanford University, where he earned his law degree in 1926. He was described as shy, charming, and a frenetic dancer, and these attributes could be seen in his mountaineering endeavors as well.[8] His father, Walter A. Starr, Sr., inspired in his oldest son a love for the mountains as deep and passionate as Clyde's. All of Pete's free time was spent in the Sierra, and his exploits were becoming legendary. He often traveled alone, covering long distances in explosive bursts. His desire to know the Sierra was so ingrained in him that he set out to convey that love, appreciation, and knowledge to others by compiling a guidebook, the first comprehensive narrative describing the John Muir Trail. It was during a stint of fieldwork in August 1933 that he met his untimely end.

According to the account published in the *Sierra Club Bulletin* for June 1934, Pete Starr left San Francisco on the evening of July 29, 1933, for an unknown destination in the Sierra. He planned to meet his father at Glacier Lodge on August 7, allowing a little more than one week to do some solitary exploring and climbing, which he greatly enjoyed. He never met up with his father, who returned to Piedmont on August 9, uneasy at the prospect of not having seen his son but nevertheless confident that he was actively engaged in some high-country pursuit. When the young Starr failed to return to work on the morning of August 14, however, his father became convinced that his son was in trouble, and he began to organize a search.

The first problem was determining where Pete had parked his car. The elder Starr knew that his son had planned on crossing the Sierra Nevada via Tioga Pass, and was therefore somewhere on the east side. The California Highway Patrol, Forest Service, State Police, and Inyo and Mono County Sheriffs Offices were given descriptions of the vehicle, and it was found that evening at Agnew Meadows, the trailhead for the Minarets region west of Mammoth and southeast of Yosemite. A pair of resident miners had also made an earlier report to the authorities on the location of Starr's abandoned camp at Lake Ediza—common knowledge in the Agnew Meadows area—but no formal action had been taken based on that tip until the search for Pete Starr was instigated by his father.[9]

Francis Farquhar came to the aid of the Starr family by contacting several Sierra Club members who were climbers and mountaineers, enlisting them for the grueling and perilous search. Clyde was at the top of Farquhar's list, but because he was in the backcountry he could not be immediately reached. From Los Angeles came Glen Dawson and Richard Jones; Jules Eichorn, Lowell Hardy, Mike Sutro, Whiting Welch, Walter Starr, Sr., and Allan Starr (Walter's son and Pete's brother) drove all night from Oakland, arriving at the Mammoth Ranger Station at 7 a.m. on the morning of August 15. A party of twelve volunteers, composed of Starr's friends, local businessmen, and others were previously dispatched by Chief Ranger Douglas Robinson for Lake Ediza at 3:30 that morning.

Meanwhile, Eichorn, Dawson, Jones, and the Starrs left for Lake Ediza from Agnew Meadows. The earlier search party was already out, combing the area in the vicinity of the lake, but because its members were not mountaineers, they stayed in the area east of the Minarets and Mt. Ritter, letting the experienced climbers concentrate on the peaks in the Ritter Range, where it was more likely that Starr would have gotten into trouble.

That evening, Clyde and Oliver Kehrlein tromped into camp, fresh from the Palisades. They were at Glacier Lodge when they heard the news, and left quickly to help with the search, making possible a fourth search party. The following morning Douglas Robinson, Jr., and Lilburn Norris of Mammoth climbed the east face of Mt. Ritter, where they found Starr's summit entry of July 31. Because Starr's ice axe and crampons were found in his camp, the searchers knew that he had made it back from Ritter safely. Walter Starr, Sr., and his son Allan climbed Banner Peak but did not find any evidence of Pete's presence on that summit. Clyde and Kehrlein searched the east and northeast sides of Clyde Minaret (then known simply as "Highest Minaret"), discovering a bit of cloth and some fresh rock piles—known as "ducks" or "cairns" and used to mark trails—that they attributed to Starr. Meanwhile, Dawson, Jones, and Eichorn approached the Minarets from the west, where they made several important finds.

. Michael Minaret was a fresh rock slide, and at the top of a
.s another series of rock ducks and a half-smoked Chesterfield
.te, Starr's preferred brand. Dawson said he and Eichorn "hur-
up Michael's Minaret, but found no evidence of anyone having
.en there since our previous climb with [Walter] Brem in 1931."[10]

The next day, August 17, Dawson and Eichorn found more evidence of Starr's presence, this time in the second chute north of
Michael's Chimney. Dawson wrote, "None of them [rock ducks] were
down. The ducks were usually of three stones, although one at the
head of the first chute north of Michael's chimney was quite large.
We saw indistinct footprints in one place. These ducks connected
with the ones we saw the day before. The line of ducks was made by
an experienced route finder. Jules and I both admired the excellence
of the route." After climbing the Third Minaret, they headed south
toward Clyde Minaret, where they met up with Clyde and Kehrlein,
who were searching near Iceberg Lake. A frustrated Dawson noted,
"We were stumped. As I write this I can't understand it. Lines of duck
led to near the summit of two major summits of the Minarets, but no
signatures on top; Starr usually wrote lengthy accounts in registers I
have seen."

Meanwhile, Farquhar was conducting a search for his friend from
the air, in the hope that an injured Starr would somehow try to sig-
nal the plane. Starr's senior law partner, Vincent Butler, had made
arrangements with Standard Oil Company for the use of their aircraft,
on which Farquhar served as passenger and lookout. He recalled, "We
flew from San Francisco over Yosemite and over around the Minarets.
I knew that the only hope of his being alive would be if he was near
water. So I examined very carefully every water course, every snow
field in the vicinity of the Minarets, but saw nothing there."[11] After
searching the area for two days the aerial approach was abandoned.
The Civilian Conservation Corps search party that had been launched
from Mammoth also returned to its camp.

One last group effort was mounted on August 18. Clyde, Dawson,
Eichorn, Jones, Kehrlein, and Walter and Allan Starr searched and
climbed the east face of Banner Peak. Afterward, the group members
left for Agnew Meadows and their respective homes. Dawson wrote,
"We seemed to give up the search rather suddenly. However, I don't
know how much value further search would be. It is like trying to find
a needle in a haystack. I urged Mr. Starr to let Clyde stay on, and I
hope the mystery may some day be solved."

Clyde continued the search by himself. He felt an obligation to help, to bring the matter to a close, so that Starr's parents would know what had happened to their son, and that his death had come swiftly.[12] Clyde deduced that Starr was not to be found on Highest Minaret, even though he believed that Starr had been on its summit although he had not left a record. He also eliminated the Minarets north of Michael's Notch, where the other rock ducks were found. Clyde focused his suspicions on Michael Minaret, the third highest peak in the chain, and after resting in camp on the 24th and giving the matter careful consideration, decided to concentrate his efforts there.[13]

Leaving camp early on the morning of the 25th Clyde climbed through Michael's Notch to the southwest side and from there gradually ascended the west face to the summit. Scanning the lesser peaks with his binoculars, he remained on the summit for half an hour before beginning his descent, all the while searching the northwest face, which he deemed "a capital place to fall."[14] Many years later Clyde told interviewer Tom Miller, "I thought, well, doggone it, he's up there somewhere. Then I heard bzzzzzzzzzzzz...bzzzzzzzzzz. Blow flies. So I took the direction the way a bee hunter does. And I climbed about 20 feet up to get enough viewpoint, and he was lying there within 150 feet. He'd almost slid off a ledge. He was lying right there right on the edge of the ledge. He did have on a white undershirt that was showing, but you could have taken that for a little bit of snow on the north side. The rest of his clothes were khaki. He probably hadn't taken the regular route."[15] It has long been believed that Pete Starr died when a large slab of rock that he was climbing hinged outward from the base. Starr was thrown free, falling more than 300 feet before landing on the narrow ledge. Although his body was by then desiccated from the exposure, the only visible injuries were to his head.[16]

Clyde made his way back to Mammoth, where he telegraphed the news to the Starrs. The story made the front page of the *San Francisco Chronicle* on Sunday, August 27. A memorial service was also held that Sunday at the Starr home in Piedmont; the Reverend Ronald Merris of St. Paul's Church presided, and Starr's law associate Vincent Butler officiated. In Clyde's papers there is a copy of the *Chronicle* article, titled "Starr Finder Mystery Man of Mountains," that had been forwarded to him by Oliver Kehrlein, on which he had written, "Whose [sic] this man of mystery? Good stuff Norman—you might play it up—O[liver] K[ehrlein]."[17]

On August 29 a funeral party consisting of Jules Eichorn, Ranger Mace, Lilburn Norris, Douglas Robinson, Jr., and Walter A. Starr, Sr., accompanied Norman Clyde to Lake Ediza, where they made a solemn camp for the evening. The next day they climbed to the west side of Michael Minaret. Clyde and Eichorn followed Starr's ducks and eventually reached the remains. In view of the witnesses, including Mr. Starr, Jules and Norman interred Pete Starr in a cleft in the rock on the narrow ledge. The task of moving the corpse into place was left to Eichorn; Clyde would not touch it unless absolutely necessary.[18] Eichorn recounted that "Clyde was a pussy cat when it came to dead bodies. He wouldn't touch them. So here I was, a young kid with this dead climber and Norman not wanting to touch it."[19] Once the body was in place, the pair gathered rocks and walled the fallen climber into his high-altitude tomb, where he still rests today. Many years later Eichorn related to Sierra wilderness photographer Claude Fiddler that Clyde wept while they worked.[20]

As in all such cases, the paperwork was dealt with promptly. Clyde was asked by the assistant comptroller of Stanford University to provide "proof of death" for a small insurance policy that Starr had taken out while a student at the school, and in which he had named Stanford the beneficiary. Clyde replied on September 20, requesting a five-dollar check for his services and offering photographs as proof of the claim. The administrator politely declined the offer of the photos, "unless the insurance company requires more information."[21]

An unsent draft of a letter dated September 24, 1933, to Starr's mother shows Clyde's awkward but genuine attempts to comfort her: "I received your letter a few days ago. I am glad that the solving of the mystery of your son's fate brought at least some semblance of relief to you. It is still a mystery, however, why must tragedies occur, especially in the case of very worthwhile young people such as your son undoubtedly was. To lose such is a loss not only to his immediate family and friends but to humanity as well. Granting even that mountain climbing may be a somewhat dangerous form of recreation, one cannot [illegible] without running the risk of incurring some hazard. The members of the search party did the best in their powers—little as that may have been—and feel sad that more could not have been done."[22]

Many years later, Clyde wrote in an unpublished article that "had it not been for the indomitable perseverance of the lone mountaineer [Clyde himself], who followed the difficult and dangerous quest day in and day out, the family and friends of the vanished young man would probably never have known what fate had befallen him; whether he had been killed almost instantaneously or whether he had met with a painful and lingering death."[23] Clyde clearly took pride in his efforts to give the Starrs this type of closure. And the Starrs, while obviously grief-stricken, were nonetheless grateful for the assistance rendered by all parties, but especially the help that they received from Clyde and Eichorn. They provided Eichorn with a scholarship to attend the University of California, Berkeley, where he studied music and earned his teaching credentials. Eichorn recalled, "The Starrs were wonderful people, and they enjoyed my coming over and talking with them. There were [two] times that Mr. Starr and I walked back to where we could see the grave, see that nothing had moved, that all the rock work we had done to keep the body in place...remained solid."[24] Jules Eichorn also provided Starr Sr. detailed information with which to complete the volume that his son had been working on at the time of his death. After the book—*Starr's Guide to the John Muir Trail and the High Sierra Region*—was printed, a special copy was reserved for Eichorn. Inside, the inscription reads, "Jules Eichorn from Walter and Carmen Starr in Grateful Remembrance of your Great Service in August 1933."[25]

Clyde was also well taken care of by the Starrs. Mr. Starr wrote to Clyde just before Christmas 1933: "Mrs. Starr is doing very well—she has a brave spirit full of faith—but of course misses her boy terribly. They were very close to each other. I am taking her to the Ranch over Christmas where we can be alone. Am sending you a box by parcels post. Please look for it."[26] According to Steve Roper, "Walter A. Starr, Sr., is said to have rewarded Clyde with a stipend for the rest of his life."[27]

Walter A. Starr, Jr.'s death in the Minarets at the age of thirty came to symbolize the ultimate sacrifice made by mountaineers and explorers of other times and places; Farquhar compared him to "Mummery, of Nanga[;] Mallory and Irvine, of Everest; and the Americans—Allen Carpe and Theodore Koven, of Mount McKinley[;] Newman Waffl, of Robson...."[28] And just as Starr's accomplishments were rightfully praised, and his bravery and vigor commended, so too were Clyde's efforts dutifully recognized in his strenuous attempts to solve the mystery surrounding Pete Starr's disappearance.

Growing Weary of Tragedy

Norman engaged in at least three more difficult and heroic searches in his career. One year after locating the body of Walter Starr, Jr., Clyde led another search party in the Ritter Range, this time looking for a married couple.

Mr. and Mrs. Conrad Rettenbacher of Hillsborough had been climbing Banner Peak when both of them fell to their deaths. The couple, who worked as domestic help in the Hillsborough home of Howard Park, was described in the *San Francisco Examiner* as "members of the San Francisco German Hiking Club and enthusiastic amateur mountaineers." The couple had attempted to climb the west face, although contemporary newspaper accounts incorrectly gave the location as the formidable east face, which was thought to be "'all but impossible' by even the most experienced alpinists" at the time.

The couple had been missing for ten days: Clyde joined the search on August 14 and found the pair after one day of searching. Anna Rettenbacher was located in a small crevasse, having fallen from a point about 1,000 feet below the summit; the body of her husband was discovered on the glacier on the peak's west side, 600 feet below that of his wife's. Several days after the harrowing double body recovery, the couple was buried together in a mountain meadow, with forest ranger Benjamin Mace officiating at the ceremony.[29]

In 1935 Clyde almost needed to be rescued himself. Along with engineer and fellow skiing enthusiast William Dulley, Clyde was wintering at Andrew's Camp on the South Fork of Bishop Creek when they decided to ski over Piute Pass. A strong storm swept over them, burying them in heavy, wet snow. After a couple of days they decided to make the trek back over the pass and return to their lodge. Dulley never made it. They had become separated by a blizzard, with Clyde going on to find refuge in a miner's cabin near Lake Sabrina, where he was sheltered but still suffering from the effects of frostbite on his fingers and toes. Clyde began the search for his friend the next day, finding Dulley's body at the lower end of Loch Leven. The veteran skier had succumbed to a stroke. Clyde said he gave a "conservative story to the Coroner jury, partly not to disparage him [Dulley]. The appreciation that I got from such a bunch of morons that usually make up local courts was a criticism of my conduct....Had Bill followed me on this side of the pass, as anyone with common sense would have done, the case would have been very different....After giving him ample opportunity of overtaking me, it was a case of completely freezing fingers—and loss—perhaps [of] feet—and possibly of there being two [deaths] instead of one." Later, Clyde sought medical treatment in Los Angeles for his frozen toes.[30] But the toll was not just physical, as he indicated to Chester Versteeg in a letter following the event, in which he admitted that he was "becoming weary of being associated with so many tragedies in the Sierra. Being in any way responsible for one is of course worse..."[31]

Several years later, following the Japanese attack on Pearl Harbor on December 7, 1941, the western United States, and California in particular, became a major staging area for the training and deployment of troops, and Clyde's talents for rescue and recovery would be recognized by the U.S. military.

On the evening of December 12, 1941, a B-18 Tow Target Det. Ship No. 12 out of March Field Army Air Base, near Riverside, was seen circling several times over Owens Valley. Established during World War I as one of California's first air bases, March Field (known today as March Air Force Base) was, in the wake of the Pearl Harbor attack, part of the mainland Air Force presence that was a critical component of the nation's defense. The plane carried Major General Herbert A. Dargue, Colonel C. W. Bundy, Lieutenant Colonel George W. Ricker, Major Hugh McCaffery, Lieutenant Homer Burns, Captain James G. Leavitt, Staff Sergeant Hoffman, and Private Van Hamm. At around 2100 hours (9 p.m.) the airplane vanished.[32]

Several individuals in Bishop and Big Pine reported seeing a light, perhaps that of a fire, several miles distant, somewhere along the eastern slope of the Sierra. That was the only clue that the Army had to go on for the search. An Army detachment arrived to scour the area north of Big Pine Creek for clues, while military planes circled overhead. Heavy winter storms, however, precluded their efforts, and the search was temporarily abandoned.

Meanwhile, Clyde was busy that winter, gathering information from eyewitnesses regarding the plane's whereabouts. He came to the conclusion that the plane had crashed near Birch Mountain, a peak 13,660 feet high, slightly east of the Sierran crest and fifteen air miles southwest of Big Pine.

Clyde waited out the winter. Around the first of May, he was approached by George Burns, father of Lieutenant Homer Burns, who had asked for Clyde's assistance. Burns had learned from a miner living in the foothills west of Bishop that he thought the plane might have tried to make a forced landing on Table Mountain, in the Bishop Creek drainage north of Big Pine Creek. Clyde climbed the mountain and skied the entire four-mile length of its summit but found nothing. The next day he climbed another 12,000 feet on the head waters of Baker Creek, where the plane may have gone down, but without success.

On May 4 Clyde ascended Kid Mountain, where he could study with his binoculars what he described as the "precipitous couloir—fluted north face of Birch Mountain and the cirque lying between the two mountains and continuing to the crest of the Sierra a short distance to the west." He carefully scrutinized the mountain "when, suddenly, as I swept my binoculars slowly along, with startling suddenness I became aware of a star coming within the field of vision. Still partially buried in snow, the vanished plane lay at an elevation of some 11,250 feet, a short distance below a tier of cliffs running along the northern base of Birch Mountain." Making careful notes of the plane's location, Clyde shouldered his rucksack and glissaded wildly down the west face of Kid Mountain and into the north fork of Big Pine Creek, walking back to Glacier Lodge, where he retired for the evening.

The next morning Clyde and Burns's brother-in-law, Albert Bergen, made their way up Birch Creek to the plane. Studying the scattered debris and crushed fuselage, it appeared to Clyde that the plane had crashed into the cliffs above its final resting place. The body of Private Van Hamm was the first to be located; the whereabouts of the others was still unknown.

That evening Clyde and Bergen met Colonel Joseph H. Davidson of March Field and reported to him their findings. The next morning a detachment of Army officers and enlisted men, led by Major William C. Evans, arrived at Big Pine for the recovery effort. They established a base camp on Birch Creek and followed a little-used trail to Birch Lake, which was still covered in five feet of ice.

The next task was to find out exactly where the plane had impacted the mountain. Clyde found that it had hit a rocky granite rib located between two snow-filled chutes, and he speculated that the plane rolled into the chute east of the rib and cartwheeled down 1,500 feet before it came to rest where he found it. Clyde later wrote, "The force of its impact had been so great that it had torn apart granite in which there are only occasional joints. Roundabout were strewn several propeller blades and other pieces of heavy mechanism [sic]. A short distance below, along the crest of the rib and partially buried in snow lay the bodies of Col. Bundy and Ricker."[33]

There remained five other bodies to recover. Clyde noted in his official report that "the rest of the occupants of the plane had apparently been hurled from it into the chute or had been carried down it and thrown from the plane at varying distances. The problem of finding these [bodies] was further complicated by the fact that during the winter…[numerous] snow slides had gone down the coulees, shot over the drop near the lower end of the latter, and debouched fan-wise from its mouth on the slope above the lake."[34] But Clyde continued to search. In an unpublished article, Clyde wrote that "at irregular intervals the bodies of the lost continued to be recovered. That of Major Hugh McCaffery was discovered in the deep snow east of the plane, and was followed the next day by that of Lt. Burns [who was spotted by his brother-in-law]. During the first week of July those of Captain James G. Leavitt and Brigadier General [sic] Herbert A. Dargue were found in the same area. There remained now only that of Sgt. Hoffman[;] where it lay there was no means of telling. It might be in the snow fan at the mouth of the chute[,] somewhere up the chute, or might even have been hurled into an adjoining one. Several weeks passed without anything being discovered."[35]

Clyde's perseverance was nothing short of heroic. Day after day he continued to look for the lost man, climbing the steep sides of the mountain and descending its narrow, ice-filled canyons. Finally, after three more weeks, Clyde located the remains of Hoffman in another chute, still buried in deep snow. Clyde concludes his essay by writing, "This search is unparalleled in the annals of those lost in the high mountains. Almost three months had elapsed from the time of the discovery of the plane and the finding of the last of its occupants. Yet, with the exception of the bodies of the two colonels lying on the granite rib just below the point where the ship had reached, in not a single case had more than two days passed between the appearance of a body above the snow and its discovery by one or other members of the Air Corps or by the writer. Usually, within a day after a hand, foot or head had begun to protrude above the snow it was detected by the ever-alert members of the party."[36]

Clyde received numerous commendations from the Army, including letters from Brigadier General B. M. Giles of the Headquarters Fourth Air Force, and Colonel Davidson. In his letter of commendation to the chief of the Army Air Forces, Colonel Davidson wrote,

"Mr. Clyde's ability to instruct others, and his leadership are of superior quality. Due to his work with the men, an excellent instructor cadre exists today for training others in like work."[37] Davidson sent a copy to Clyde, saying, "You are welcome to use the enclosure in support of your offer of assistance to the army, which I understand you are making."[38] In addition to the commendations, the Army gave Clyde enough campaign hats to last him a lifetime, and an ample supply of military clothing that he wore for many years.[39]

While Clyde may have made a bid to the Army to train young recruits, he was not selected for the job. The Army utilized younger men with perhaps greater skills in technical climbing, like David Brower, to fill out the ranks of the elite Tenth Mountain Division. Jules Eichorn was himself hired by the National Park Service in Yosemite to train the rangers in climbing and rescue techniques. Eichorn later recalled, "I started the rescue team. [Francis] Farquhar was Sierra Club president and my friend. He recommended [me] to the Park Service, and we started in 1941. Before[, they] had no rangers trained to handle high angle climbing, and no equipment. They knew they had a problem, but didn't know how to solve it. With our techniques we could climb from the floor of the valley. We developed an efficient rescue technique so it was possible to rescue from the bottom, from any face."[40]

While Brower, Richard Leonard, Art Argiewicz,[41] Harold Kirker, and other Sierra Club members were serving in the Armed Forces during World War II, and Eichorn was training the rangers in Yosemite, Clyde performed yet another rescue that has been called the greatest in American mountaineering to that time. He was climbing North Palisade in August 1943 with two aircraft engineers, Harlow Russ and Herschel Asbury, when they were caught in a crushing rockfall 250 feet from the summit. Clyde and Russ were unhurt, but Asbury was swept screaming over a cliff. His leg was broken, a hand was crushed, and he suffered severe head trauma. Clyde stabilized the injured man, secured both he and Russ to the steep, narrow ledge where Asbury had landed, and, leaving the two men to comfort one another through the night, left on his perilous descent. Upon reaching Glacier Lodge (a distance of eight miles) he telephoned the Forest Service and told them of Asbury's grave condition. He gathered up food, clothing, and blankets for the men, and at dawn proceeded to make the steep and strenuous climb back to their airy bivouac site. He then climbed back down, met the search and rescue party, and led them to his companions.

The fifty-eight-year-old Clyde wasn't done yet. He directed every aspect of the rescue, helping to lower the injured man in a Stokes rescue litter from the mountainside to the glacier, and then carrying Asbury across the glacier to a waiting mule, which transported him to a hospital. Asbury lost one finger in the mishap and suffered a limp as a result of his broken leg, but credits Clyde with saving his life.[42]

Clyde was involved in at least one other rescue, at the age of sixty-five, when he assisted the Inyo County Sheriffs Department with a search and rescue operation on Mt. Whitney in the summer of 1950.[43] Two young men, Christopher Smith Reynolds and Steve Wasserman, were eager to climb the east face, although they were lacking in mountaineering experience. They had hired Clyde to be their guide, but he was one day late in returning to Lone Pine to accompany them on their climb, so the pair attempted the ascent without assistance, and with disastrous results. Several days later Clyde located their broken bodies on the talus slopes of the great peak. It must have been especially difficult for Clyde, who had pioneered the original route up the east face nineteen years earlier with two young men not unlike Reynolds and Wasserman. Clyde knew that his articles about mountaineering appealed to a wide audience, and the romance and drama of climbing attracted young men eager for adventure. Finding two more victims in his beloved Sierra must have been a sad experience for him, especially as he was nearing the end of his own career as a climber.[44]

Since World War II there has been an explosion in the number of visits to the nation's national parks and forests, and a corresponding increase in the number of injured and lost hikers and climbers. Historian Roderick Nash attributes the growth of mountaineering to a number of factors, including advances in transportation, available information, and equipment.[45] Prior to the war, a relatively small group of individuals engaged in wilderness travel—usually members of the Sierra Club, who organized large trips complete with pack trains, canned goods, and bulky tents, bedrolls, and clothing. Technological advances brought on by the war effort enabled more people to spend longer periods of time in the wilderness, traveling faster and lighter than their predecessors, but also increasing their chances of getting into trouble, unable to extricate themselves from dangerous situations. As backpackers and climbers push themselves and their equipment to the limits of their endurance and beyond, rescuers have to respond in kind, often putting themselves in great danger; the Forest Service, Park Service, County Sheriffs, Highway Patrol, and even the military are often called upon to search for the lost, the injured, and the dead. Of course, the cost of these operations can be enormous, especially in times of government cutbacks, and there exists a philosophical debate regarding the limits of the government's responsibility for rescuing or recovering individuals who go beyond the limits of their strength, skills, abilities, or common sense. Nevertheless, today's search and rescue rangers are direct descendants of Norman Clyde in their dedication and devotion to their mission of aiding wilderness travelers.[46]

CHAPTER 8

The Occasional Hilarious Indulgence: Naturalist, Guide, and Friend

Norman Clyde's training as a naturalist began early in his life. His boyhood spent in the forests and fields of western Pennsylvania and Canada honed his skills as an outdoorsman. He became an astute observer of wildlife, and learned the flora of the various places he would live in and explore throughout his life. His formal education also prepared him for nature study as his coursework at Geneva College included classes in biology, chemistry, geology, and physics. From 1943 until his death Clyde also served as a member of and wildlife observer for the California Academy of Sciences, based in San Francisco.[1]

That, combined with a lifetime of experience in the outdoors, made him a valuable source of information about the natural history of his high-elevation abode.

During the course of his lifetime Clyde became acquainted with several scientists, both through his work with the Sierra Club and just by living in the mountains he called home. One of the most prominent of this distinguished group was Joseph Grinnell, director of the Museum of Vertebrate Zoology at the University of California, Berkeley. In a 1928 article in *The Auk*, the journal of the American Ornithologists' Union, Grinnell described a previously unknown subspecies of screech owl found by Clyde near Independence. Clyde discovered the nesting pair the previous fall and, in the fashion of the time, shot them for the purpose of collecting them as specimens. There had previously been no record of screech owls east of the Sierra divide, north from Latitude 35 to Lake Tahoe, a discovery which, Grinnell wrote, "[made] possible the characterization of the new subspecies."[2]

In other correspondence between the two, Clyde related the harrowing tale of his encounter with a wolverine: "On August 12, [1925,] as I was going from Colby Meadow to Evolution Basin, a wolverine came running down the trail. Evidently it did not see me, or thought that it had the right of way, as it came up to within six or eight [yards] of me. However, as I held my ground and was fumbling around in my lunch bag for an automatic [handgun] I had with me, the animal changed its mind and ran rapidly away for some forty yards, then turned to scan me for a few seconds, disappearing finally among rocks before I could get a shot at it."[3] According to Harold E. Crowe, Clyde always carried a gun on the Sierra High Trips, specifically in the event of an encounter with a wolverine. Crowe stated that Clyde "felt that this was the one dangerous thing [animal]" to be encountered in the wild.[4] In a January 1938 article that appeared in the magazine *Fur-Fish-Game* Clyde related a story of marten trapping in the Sierra. He accompanied Leo Castagno, an employee of the Southern Sierra Power Company, on a ski patrol of his traplines. On this particular trip they did not find any martens in the traps, although Castagno did indicate where he had in the past caught marten, white weasel, and even a bobcat. Clyde welcomed the opportunity to strap on the boards and look for wildlife at the same time.[5]

Clyde also enjoyed learning the flowers. He sprinkled into his various articles on climbing descriptions of the flora he found in the Sierra, and much to the delight of his companions, he always knew where the good berries could be found before and after an ascent. He also wrote extensively on the plant and animal life of the eastern Sierra, penning numerous articles on birds, flowers, insects, and wildlife. His observances of wildlife were sometimes close at hand, as he once had a ringtail cat take up residence in his cabin; the alert and intelligent animal would sometimes engage in a tumultuous game of blind man's bluff directly above Clyde's bed in the wee hours of the morning. Clyde didn't begrudge the animal its "occasional hilarious indulgences" because it was an excellent mouser who kept his cabin free of vermin, of which there was an endless supply. Clyde enjoyed placing food outside his cabin for the various birds and animals that lived in the region, including the ringtail cat and Douglas squirrel.

One endearing story that Clyde wrote was about his relationship with the small chickadees that visited him in the winter: "During one winter I often fed them peanut kernels. When, as I sometimes did, reclined in the sunshine on the south side of the cabin, I occasionally scattered peanut kernels about my person, chickadees were soon alighting all over me, gleefully picking them up and carrying them away to be devoured on some nearby branch. It was not long before I could scarcely emerge from my cabin without being followed by chickadees. Occasionally I placed peanut kernels on my hat. As I walked or skied along, the chickadees continued to alight on it until the supply of these was exhausted."[6]

His naturalist abilities served him in other, more practical ways as well. Clyde spent long periods of time alone in the mountains and needed to either carry his food with him or secure it along the way. Because he was always armed, he could also shoot game for food when the need and the opportunity arose. One of his favorite pastimes was fishing, and his unrivalled knowledge of the Sierra led him to many isolated stretches of river where he utilized his superb climbing skills to access deep, fish-filled pools. There he would cast his fly onto the calm waters, often catching his limit of Loch Leven, rainbow, or golden trout in short order. The fish he caught were often huge by today's standards; Clyde wrote of catching trout that averaged eighteen inches in length, and sometimes upward of two feet long. Fish smaller than twelve inches were returned to the water. Given his prodigious appetite, all of the fish he procured were eaten, usually on the same day or the following morning, as adequate storage and refrigeration were unavailable. In a piece about a backpacking trip across the Sierra one fall, Clyde wrote, "On the first day of October, despite my having eaten an almost unbelievable number of them during the summer in my solitary rambling, I felt that I would relish a mess of trout." He caught his limit of fifteen that day, in the Grand Canyon of the Kings River.[7]

Clyde, of course, would not readily disclose his favorite fishing haunts. He did, however, acknowledge the areas of which he was particularly fond: a tributary of the Middle Fork of the Kings River, another feeder stream on the South Fork of the Kings, the Grand Canyon of the Tuolumne, and Bubbs Creek. It was on these rugged, seldom traveled stretches of water-filled gorges that he would climb, jump, and scramble, threading his way along narrow ledges to reach the quiet pools full of trout. As he wrote many years ago, "To the agile trout fisherman it is indeed a thrill to leap about our great blocks of granite, climb around numerous cascades, and sometimes spring from rock to rock in the roaring spring itself in his quest for these superb golden trout."[8]

As Smoke Blanchard, a mountaineer, climbing guide, and longtime friend of Clyde's, recalled many years later, "Norman spent all his time in the mountains and was as deeply into fishing as into any other aspect of life in the wild....He would not fish unless they were biting. He would lie all afternoon in the sun reading Dumas in French, gazing out across the lake to check for ripples, and when he thought there was enough breeze on the surface for fly fishing, he would be off for one circuit of the lake and would return with his limit of Golden Trout."[9]

Norman fished for food; he was not a sport fisherman, nor did he fish simply to while away the time. It was a serious pursuit and one he took seriously. Fishing to him meant fishing with a fly rod and reel, and no bait—he was a purist in the purest sense of the word.

Trail Crew Member and Guide

From time to time Norman would pick up work as a government employee. It is not known why he accepted these occasional seasonal occupations; perhaps it was for the money, or to explore some favorite part of the Sierra at length while his meals were provided. Whatever the reason, his stints at regular federal government employment were apparently few and far between, and those that he did engage in were most likely not for pleasure but out of necessity; it doesn't appear that he enjoyed himself.

One of his earliest government endeavors was working as a trail crew member in Sequoia National Park in the early 1930s. Clyde was part of the enormous effort to build the High Sierra Trail, which linked Giant Forest on the west side of the park with Mt. Whitney, along the eastern crest. Clyde called it "one of the most remarkable trails in the United States...some seventy miles of trans-Sierra trail, contouring along granite cliffs, climbing high passes and descending into deep canyons in its various course. [The trail] intersects most of the other trails of the great mountain hinterland of the Sequoia National Park in such a way that almost any place in it accessible by trail can be reached without difficulty, merely by leaving the 'trunk' trail...and proceeding north or south from it. This enables one to 'circle' around almost at will in the great 'back country' of the park."[10]

The work was hard, heavy, and hazardous; injuries were frequent and problematic given the isolation and long distances to medical facilities. Minor injuries were treated onsite whereas more serious cases required transport out of the backcountry over distances of up to forty miles, an arduous undertaking for the victim as well as the rescuers.[11] Clyde injured his back while working on the trail in October 1932, and although the nature, severity, and cause of the injury is not known, there is record of his having filed a claim with the United States Employees' Compensation Commission, which, when it finally responded to him more than a year later, disallowed his claim, stating, "The fact that an injury was sustained in the performance of duty is not established."[12]

Clyde exploded in anger. He received the letter in Bishop, and responded with the following tirade:

> My veracity has never been questioned and only [by] an aggregation of imbeciles such as this...commission has shown itself to be. Bogus accounts of injuries have been sent in, but the commission has neither the intelligence nor the information necessary to distinguish the true from the false in such cases.
>
> It might be enlightening to your block-headed aggregation to be informed that I have gone for upwards of 48 hours without sleep in rescuing the injured and the dying, and that I have continued, time and again, the search for the lost in the mountains after all others have quit, and that I eventually succeeded in my quest. Then when I receive an injury my word and report is rejected by an outfit of ignorant morons masquerading as a commission, for whom a man of the mountains has nothing but contempt and scorn. Yours Truly, Norman Clyde.[13]

It would be almost ten years before Norman would work for the federal government again. This time the U.S. Geological Survey, whose members were conducting a resurvey of the Goddard quadrangle in the southern Sierra Nevada, invited him. They hired Norman to help carry their survey equipment up Mt. Darwin and some of the other peaks in the Evolution Basin. It was during World War II, the Sierra Club was on hiatus during the war, and Norman didn't have any other means of support, so he agreed. In his account of the trip he showed a rare sense of humor as he described the mule that he was assigned: "To my astonishment I was introduced to what was supposed to be my mount, a bone rack of a mule about seven feet high and so old that he was about ready to drop over dead. At the sight of this animated carcass ready for the bone yard, I ejaculated, 'why didn't the packer on Big Pine Creek send a saw horse?' On my way, I eventually succeeded in dragging my moribund mount over Bishop Pass, 12,000'." Clyde and his mule, "at a rate of speed slightly greater than absolute motionless," made their way through the Sierra one more time; no doubt both man and animal complained bitterly along the way.[14]

Following World War II, Jules Eichorn organized a "cache and carry" trip for boys fourteen to sixteen years old to experience the Sierra firsthand. The trips emphasized fishing, climbing, and camp craft, and included several adult leaders, among them Norman Clyde and Dave Brower's younger brother Joe. Eichorn's reasoning was simple and direct: foremost, he felt that time spent in the mountains was an invaluable experience for young people. Because he himself had gotten so much out of his years of climbing and hiking he wanted to share some of those experiences with others, including his own children. As a music teacher, Eichorn wasn't saddled with correcting papers or preparing exams, so he spent his weekends and summers either in the Sierra Nevada or planning trips to the mountains. As he recalled many years later,

I wanted to see more of the Sierra, and I couldn't afford, being married, to go off by myself. [The cache and carry trips] gave me an opportunity to take a bunch of boys for a month, and really give them a feel [for the mountains]. And I got to plan a trip, so I was doing it for selfish reasons as well. Each year I'd take a different section of the Sierra that I hadn't seen, and plan the trip there. I did this for about five years. I knew the packers, and would say to Charley Robinson, 'I want my caches placed here, here, here, and here. One hundred yards off the trail he would place wooden pack boxes bound with wire, which made it difficult for bears and other animals to break into. I would pack all the food here [at his home in Redwood City]. I had a 1931 straight-eight Packard and a box trailer on a Model T chassis to haul the food boxes.

I asked Norman Clyde to help me. In case of emergency he would be the perfect person to help out, and secondly he was a magnificent fisherman. He was willing to show them how to cast a fly; bait fishing was a travesty to Norman, who would adamantly state "it's not a sport!"

I told the boys, they're not to touch any of Norman's gear or equipment at all, ever, because he was so fussy. He had a 3/4 Hudson Bay axe; he kept it so sharp you could shave with it. One kid picked it up one time and foolishly tried to chop with it while Norman was off fishing, and he nicked the axe. Norman was furious about it. He almost came apart. The kid got hell from me, too. Things turned out all right, he spent 1/2 hour getting the nick out.

I was climbing then. Yes, we did some climbs. We wouldn't do difficult ones. There are so many marvelous peaks, the views, you'd just be careful not to roll rocks on anyone.

He was also an interesting person to talk to. The boys could learn a lot from a mature man who knew what he wanted to do and what he didn't. Anybody who could live in the mountains the way Norman did and not have to depend on someone else, that was really something.[15]

In contrast to his cameraderie with Eichorn, Clyde could also be wary and aloof with his fellow mountaineers, perhaps in keeping with his competitive nature. During the war, Paul and Mary DeDecker encountered Clyde in the backcountry. The DeDeckers were on a backpacking trip down the John Muir Trail with family and their friend Art Reyman, who made it a hobby to climb peaks (for first ascents) that nobody else seemed to want to climb. Clyde joined his friends the DeDeckers and Reyman one evening at their campfire. Both Clyde and Reyman knew of one another, but they maintained a "very cool" distance the entire evening, not wanting to acknowledge the accomplishments and exploits of the other.[16]

Another close friendship that Clyde had was with the artist Robert Clunie. A decade younger than Clyde, Clunie was a native of Scotland, where his father had been head gamekeeper for the Gilmore estate in Eaglesham, Renfrewshire. When Robert was fourteen the family immigrated to the United States, settling in Saginaw, Michigan, where he landed his first art job, at the age of eighteen, decorating farm machinery. Five years later he was in California painting movie scenery for Metro Studios. Later, as a resident of the Ventura County town of Santa Paula, Clunie supported himself for years as a housepainter while he pursued his art.

During the summers Clunie would head for the high mountains of the American West. His favorite areas included the Grand Tetons of Wyoming and the Sierra Nevada range. Beginning in 1930 and continuing until the late 1960s Clunie spent a total of sixty months in a camp located below the North Palisade, on the headwaters of Big Pine Creek between Fourth and Fifth Lakes at an elevation of 11,000 feet. It was there that he painted the spectacular scenery of the High Sierra and developed an intimate connection with the region. During this time he also came to know the Palisade region as well as anyone, including Clyde, and his camp was often sought out by prominent businessmen, writers, and scientists, who enjoyed the artist's company as well as his skill not only with a paintbrush but with a fishing rod.

Clyde wrote about his summertime high-country companion, lavishing him with praise—something that Clyde rarely did. Clyde recounted that "painting the mountains and the lakes [was] not...the only interest" of the artist; Clunie spent at least a portion of every day' fishing for trout, some of which he shared with his neighbors, Clyde included. Further, the mountaineer marveled that "it is not necessary that he spend very much time fishing, for he knows where, when and how to catch them. The result of this knowledge and skill is that in a half hour of fishing he catches more trout than the average angler visiting the lakes does in a half-day or more. Robert Clunie is a sufficiently expert fisherman to hook, play and land almost all of the trout that takes his lures. He uses flies, bait and occasionally lures. Being an artist he can kill two birds with one stone, for, while he is enjoying his fishing in a more or less stationary position he can at the same time observe the continually changing play of lights and shades on the lakes, on the rolling terrain dotted with pine trees around them and the lofty mountains by which the amphitheater is surrounded."[17]

The two men shared a common philosophy as well. They shared a love of the mountains and each tried, in their own way, to capture the essence of their meaning and give it expression in their life work. Clunie's words, which follow, could well be Clyde's:

In the mountains there is an education from the Master Artist in the creation of the universe. The stronger and more bold the composition of the mountains, the gentler the flowers and ferns. Without balance there is nothing at all. The world is so perfectly balanced that it is an example of perfection. I find perfection here and my job is to try, if possible, to interpret it in a personal way. The search is its own reward. It is not necessary that people accept your paintings. The essential thing is to find truth.[18]

Clunie also had some kind words for Clyde: "I've analyzed Norman's beefs against humanity, and I've found that he's always basically right. He's a perfectionist, a dreamer. He's a great mountaineer."[19]

CHAPTER 9

On Top of the World: Honors, Recognition, and Awards

For someone reputed to have been a "recluse," Norman Clyde received recognition and accolades in many forms throughout his long life, and what's more, he appeared to enjoy them. In the biography he wrote for *Who's Who*, he listed his many awards and even used the honorary title "Doctor of Science," which had been bestowed upon him by his alma mater.

A large part of Clyde's recognition came about through the many newspaper and magazine articles written about him and his exploits, beginning as early as 1923, when the National Park Service boasted of his endeavors while climbing in Glacier National Park. The April 1928 issue of *National Motorist* included a full-length article, written by Neill C. Wilson, entitled "A Prodigious Climber of Mountains: This Is the Title Given to Norman Clyde who Takes his Mild Exercise by Scaling Peaks." The article gives grand praise to the schoolteacher/ mountaineer, and includes a photo of the campaign hat–holding Clyde dressed in high boots, jodhpurs, and wearing a backpack. His countenance is serious, his stance relaxed. That piece would be followed by numerous articles in newspapers and magazines over the next forty-four years and beyond.

It's hard to say what Clyde thought of all of this. He didn't exactly shrink away from the publicity, but neither does it appear that he consciously sought it out. He was most interested in relating tales and stories of the mountains, and seemed antagonistic when it came to anything approaching a biographical sketch. His personal feelings about publishing are reflected in his correspondence with friends. H. L. Branthaver recounted Clyde's feelings about selling his articles when he wrote to Clyde, "You come again with the statement that as you do not tell beautiful lies and pipe-clay and gold your articles; because you do not truckle to the depraved tastes of those who want romance and not fact, etc. etc. that your writings are not in as great demand as you might wish."[1] It remains, however, that Clyde was perhaps a little too factual in his writing, a tad Victorian and prosaic for the average reader. According to the venerable climber and author Steve Roper, "Clyde wrote relatively little of merit. His articles, devoid of personal touches and almost unendurably dull, rarely mention his companions or his inner thoughts."[2]

Clyde was sensitive about his writing and once even took umbrage at some minor criticism that his own sister offered him. In her reply, Clara Clyde Tomkies assures her brother, "You misunderstood my letter. I was not criticizing your mountain climbing. How can I do [that] intelligently when I have never climbed even one?...You see I have not outgrown my teaching habit. Most of my ten years of teaching were spent in teaching English so I only meant it as a constructive criticism. You had the material but I didn't think you displayed it to the best advantage....Please don't get angry for I am only trying to help. I have seen some of your writing that was very good and I wish the rest would be as well edited."[3]

Clyde need not have felt bad, however. Despite his grousing, he was successful in publishing several dozens of his articles in a variety of magazines and newspapers. Phil Townsend Hanna, the peripatetic editor of *Touring Topics/Westways*, published at least thirty of his articles. The *Sierra Club Bulletin* and the *American Alpine Journal* also ran his pieces, as did the *National Motorist* and *American Banker*. Although his writing may have been somewhat dry, his subjects were fresh and exciting.

Clyde's first foray into the wider world of publishing occurred as early as 1931, when he began work on a book-length project for Stanford University Press. At the time, Stanford had published several volumes of regional interest, including *Grand Canyon Country* (1929), *Big Trees* (1930), and *Death Valley* (1930) and Clyde was approached to produce a similar volume on the High Sierra; for unknown reasons it never came to fruition.[4]

The idea of authoring a book, however, never left Clyde, although it took another thirty years before Walt Wheelock, a retired Glendale police officer, worked with the aging mountaineer to compile a collection of mountaineering essays. Wheelock, "looking for things to do" upon his retirement from the police department after twenty-seven years on the force, established La Siesta Press in 1962, and *Close Ups of the High Sierra* was his first title. (This *Close Ups* is related to but not to be confused with the "'Close Ups' of Our High Sierra" series of articles Clyde wrote for *Touring Topics* in 1928. The former includes the four articles that comprised the latter, with the addition of other previously published articles as well as autobiographical, biographical, and bibliographical material compiled by Walt Wheelock.)

Wheelock had never climbed or even hiked with Clyde. Rather, Wheelock's connection to the mountaineer was through his girlfriend, Anne Adler, with whom Clyde was friends. According to Wheelock, "One of my attributes was in the field of interrogation (getting information from subjects who did not want to give it out). With this background, I was able to get Clyde to tell me things that he had always refused to discuss, such as his short-lived marriage."[5] Wheelock's efforts culminated in the first time that a simple, eloquent biography of the Old Gaffer (a nickname Clyde gave himself in his later years) found its way into print.[6] Previous articles on Clyde, which had appeared in *Fortnight* (June-July 1957), *Time* (June 20, 1960), and the ubiquitous *Reader's Digest* (October 1963) all concentrated on his climbing exploits (and, by that point, his remarkable longevity); Wheelock was the first to crack the seemingly impenetrable shell of Clyde's private life.

Perhaps as a result of the publication of *Close Ups,* yet another *Los Angeles Times* article appeared on Clyde, this one entitled "Grizzled Mountaineer 'On Top of the World.'" Accompanied by a photograph of the "legendary figure relaxing at Sierra Club base camp after leading an all-day jaunt over the crest of California's most rugged mountain range," the article gives a succinct yet complete summation of his life. Clyde provided some priceless quotes, such as, "I sort of went off on a tangent from civilization and never got back," and "I don't go in for this fad of going light. I can't be bothered with cutting a half ounce here or there, but I don't carry canned goods." The unattributed author of the article goes on to state, "Not since the time of John Muir has anyone established such a kinship with the mountain range....Clyde still roams the wilderness alone. Long ago, he lost fears acquired by the average man for lonely routes over summits and down sheer walls of granite. Somewhere along the way there's a place to find shelter, catch a few trout, munch from his 'squirrel lunch,' or just wait until the weather clears. For Norman Clyde, 50 years of rambling has been a pastime—not a hardship."[7]

Clyde made further attempts to publish his work. He met with local author and historian Dorothy Cragen of Independence, California, in February 1964 to discuss a possible monograph concerning the eastern Sierra. In a long letter dated February 27, 1964, which shows a thorough if fussy train of thought, Clyde wrote,

In thinking over the matter, the county supervisors, if interested in the publication of such material, would be interested primarily in the publicity which valley and county would receive from it. With this in mind it would seem best to confine the material to the crest of the southern Sierra from Mt. Langley north to Red Slate Mountain on the headwaters of Convict Creek, the northern terminus of that portion of the range. Perhaps an article on the John Muir trail running a short distance to the west of the crest of the southern Sierra might be included. I shall try to get together a series of accounts of ascents of the outstanding peaks of the southern Sierra beginning with Mt. Langley (perhaps) and including Mt. Whitney, Mt. Russell, Mt. Williamson, University Peak, Split Mountain (perhaps), the Middle Palisade, Mt. Sill, the North Palisade, Mt. Winchell (perhaps), Mt. Agassiz, one or two peaks on the headwaters of Bishop Creek, Mt. Humphreys, perhaps something on the headwaters of Pine Creek, Bear Creek Spire, or those of Rock Creek, Red Slate Mountain or those of Convict Creek.

Something might be given to the amphitheater on the headwaters of a number of the streams east of the crest, as these as a rule are not only surrounded by imposing peaks, but generally contain a number of fine lakes and are accessible by good trails and in one or two cases by roads. These would include that of Lone Pine Creek, Independence Creek (not very much of an amphitheater), Big Pine Creek, Bishop Creek, Pine Creek (possibly), Rock Creek, Convict Creek.

I shall try to get together a series of accounts of the ascents of the outstanding peaks, all of which have something of the dramatic in them, or at least something especially significant to them....In the accounts of the mountain ascents I shall attempt to have more or less of narrative intended [sic]. Perhaps, however, a few primarily didactic on subjects which there has been little published or that which have been published in more or less erroneous [sic] might be included. This is particularly true of the glaciers of the Sierra, especially those of the Sierra Palisades.

A book made up of such [illegible] should have considerably more of a general interest than "Close Ups" [the book]...if the material should seem of sufficient interest to justify this venture, perhaps forty or fifty [articles] would form something really worthwhile.

The above, of course, are merely some of my "cogitations."[8]

Clyde followed up with Cragen in the fall:

...wondering whether there has been any development in the publication project which you have in mind....I have heard nothing further from [publisher] Prentice-Hall, but am afraid that the matter may have come to an "impasse" as they want one sort of book and I another. I am actually afraid to turn the manuscript over to them, as an obnoxious provision in the contract empowers them to do pretty much as they please with it, once they get a hold of it. Basically they want an autobiography.

Although I am primarily interested in a mountain book, I am not opposed to a proper sort of biography, but as I have repeatedly told them, I have done little that is unusual or significant outside of my mountaineering and general wilderness experiences and these would be given more or less fully in the text in one way or another. I have, however, succeeded in getting little or nothing from them in the way of suggestions that would be worthwhile to me. It appears to me that they merely want to get hold of the material, do as they please with it and come out with a "hopped up" story, the mere sight of which would make me furious.[9]

Clyde continued to search out markets for his writings. In a letter to Katherine G. Connable, with the Eastern California Museum in Independence, Clyde wrote, "I have never had much to do with newspapers, but am supposed to be a correspondent for the *Fresno Bee*. I do not, however, know what happens in the Owens Valley, and perhaps I do not very much care. They have, however, published perhaps as many as forty articles. Recently they published two short wildlife articles out of a few [illegible] articles which I sent them. Whether they will use any more, I do not know."[10] Longtime *Fresno Bee* journalist

Gene Rose recalls, "Clyde had a perceived friendship with the *Bee*'s old 'Valley' editor Gilmore Gilbert. It was an unusual arrangement in that Gilbert was a deskbound Casper Milktoast [sic]—an indoors person as much as Clyde was an outdoor person. Gilbert's idea of climbing was the dozen or so steps to the newsroom. In Clyde he saw an individual he always wanted to be, that is, a recognized and admired outdoors person. Opposites do attract; but then Gilbert held the purse strings for free-lance writers and correspondents. And Clyde was no dummy. Gilbert accepted Clyde's articles at the going rate of a penny a word, which, I believe, was upped to two cents after the paper got some positive feedback on articles."[11]

Clyde came close to producing the book he wanted in 1965, when he began a collaboration with Sierra Club Executive Director David Brower. By that time, Clyde had written hundreds of pages of material for a book and was no doubt anxious to see his work published. Brower's troubles with the board of the Sierra Club, however, were in full swing; differences over publications, environmental matters, and the overall direction of the conservation organization resulted in Brower's resignation in 1969, leaving Clyde's book unfinished.

In the spring of 1970 two of Clyde's closest companions, Smoke Blanchard and Jules Eichorn, persuaded author Dave Bohn to work with their elderly friend on his book. The two men met, conferred on the scope and trajectory of the work, and shook hands on the agreed-to final product. Both Blanchard and Eichorn contributed pieces to the volume, describing their relationships to the Old Gaffer and offering their own insights into his life, personality, and accomplishments, and Bohn finished the volume with an epilogue describing its genesis.[12] Scrimshaw Press published *Norman Clyde of the Sierra Nevada: Rambles Through the Range of Light* in November 1971. It was, and continues to be, Norman Clyde's shining literary legacy. Noel Young Press of Santa Barbara printed three thousand copies; five hundred were handbound in Los Angeles by Earle Gray. The book contains a map of the Sierra and several photos of Clyde taken by Cedric Wright, Francis Farquhar, and Dave Bohn, among others. A handful of images taken by Clyde of his favorite peaks round out the book. Mary DeDecker recalls that the last time she saw her friend was at a book signing party at the Rocking K Ranch near Bishop, home of famed skier Jill Kinmont. Clyde spoke at the event, and Mary recalled, "It was the nicest farewell I can think of. He was shining clean, his cheeks were rosy, he was wonderful." He didn't say anything bitter or cynical;

he was pleased and proud of his lifelong work, and the book that had finally come to fruition.[13]

Glen Dawson's last contact with Clyde was arranging for a book signing at the Los Angeles bookstore that still bears the Dawson family name. Clyde was ill and could not make the trip, so the Dawsons sent a box of books up to Owens Valley for Clyde to sign. Clyde dutifully did so, inscribing each volume with the words "Verg Heil, Norman Clyde."[14]

A few years after Clyde's death, a second volume of his writings appeared, this one limited in both scope and number of copies. Glen Dawson collaborated with Edwin Carpenter in the Baja California Travel Series published by Dawson's Book Shop. Together they produced *El Picacho Del Diablo: The Conquest of Lower California's Highest Peak, 1932 and 1937*, by Norman Clyde. Noted author John W. Robinson penned the introduction and compiled the bibliography; the book was printed by Grant Dahlstrom at the Castle Press in Pasadena, and was limited to five hundred copies. The book contains several photos taken during the two expeditions to the rugged mountain peak, and includes articles written by Clyde and published in *Touring Topics* (1932) and *Westways* (1937).

Awards

Despite his isolation and distance from the major population centers of California and the United States, Clyde did receive several important accolades during his lifetime. The first, and perhaps most important, was his receipt of an honorary Doctor of Science degree from his alma mater, Geneva College, in 1939. The college later gave him another honor, a Distinguished Service Award, in 1962. In both instances he went to western Pennsylvania to receive these honors, traveling round-trip by bus. He appeared to have been genuinely thrilled by the honorary doctorate; afterward he was often referred to in correspondence as "Dr. Clyde," and he signed his articles "Norman Clyde, D.Sc." By contrast, the Distinguished Service Award was something of a disappointment to him, as it was given in honor of his nature writings and not his many other accomplishments.[15]

Clyde's relationship with the Sierra Club, which might be expected to have been a source of accolades, was more complex. According to Ted Waller, Clyde's "personality conflicts" with High Trip leaders and the Sierra Club elite made his dealings with them difficult.[16] He served on the Sierra Club Committee for Mountain Records for a time (along with Jules Eichorn, Oliver Kehrlein, Glen Dawson, Helen LeConte, Richard Leonard, and others), however, Clyde was a nonconformist and not a part of the social crowd that dominated the leadership of the club. Although he was a great asset in the mountains, he could be stubborn and difficult to get along with, traits reflected in an April 23, 1939, letter to Francis Farquhar from Hervey H. Voge, in which Voge discusses the naming of a peak for Clyde:

Dear Francis:

Dave Brower has informed me that you are opposed to our suggestion to name Peak 13,956 *Mount Clyde*. I find it rather difficult to understand your hesitation, and I would like to know whether you feel Clyde unworthy of the honor. Personally, I can see quite a few reasons why Clyde should be given a peak, and very few objections. The reasons are:

There is no other man who knows the High Sierra better or who loves it more dearly.

He has done much through writing and example to spread a true appreciation of nature.

He has always been glad to help others, and to share every phase of mountaineering with them.

He has practiced and promulgated the highest ideals of the alpinist: courage, care, courtesy, modesty, friendliness.

His contribution to the cause of conservation is noteworthy.

My own respect for Norman Clyde is based on more than three weeks of climbing with him, on what I have heard from others, on impressions from his letters, and on his writings. He represents in many ways an ideal: the active intellectual man. For while he takes great pleasure in the physical activity of climbing (which we all understand), he at the same time never abandons his more intellectual interests. He has a broad knowledge of botany, geology, and wild-life; he also is deeply interested in philology and classical philosophy.

One of the most amazing things about Clyde is his retirement from normal social and economic life. It is hard to convince oneself what great courage and what great love of the outdoor life are necessary for the successful accomplishment of such a retirement. It is even more amazing that Norman has done it without becoming "queer." I think that this fact alone is a very good indication of his character.

That other people appreciate Clyde is attested by the forthcoming degree of Doctor of Science, which Geneva College is to confer on him this summer.

To tell the truth, the custom of naming peaks after mortal men does not please me. How much happier the situation in the Alps! But the damage has been done in the Sierra, and the best that we can now do is to see that the peaks bear the names of men who are somehow related to mountains or to people who love the mountains. I think that this has been the policy of the [Sierra] club, though the club may have gone too far in honoring men who were of interest to club members only. But in Clyde we have a man who belongs less to the club than to all people who love the mountains and the beauties of untrammeled nature.

I am very anxious that you give this matter your serious consideration, since you are in the position of a censor. And if you decide against naming Peak 13,956 Mt. Clyde, please let me know immediately, so that I can take action as I think most fitting....

P.S. I fear I haven't emphasized above the most important reason for honoring Clyde with a peak. That is his outstanding record as a climber. It appears unlikely that anyone else will ever climb the Sierra peaks to the extent that Norman has. And he has never done so as a matter of establishing records or of getting prestige. His behavior there contrasts with that of the less pure devotees of the art; while we boast of our few mediochre [sic] climbs, he does not even bother to record his many ascents. I have often seen him fail to sign the register on top of a peak simply because he was not interested in such things. HHV[17]

The U.S. Board on Geographic Names ultimately accepted the recommendation and bestowed Norman Clyde's name on the peak (and its glacier) in 1973 and 1974, respectively. Other features in the Sierra include Clyde Minaret, Clyde Spires, Clyde Meadow, and Clyde's Ledge.[18]

Clyde's tempestuous relationship with the Sierra Club continued through the 1950s, as evidenced by an exchange of letters that began with one from Winifred Thompson to Kathy Jackson. Thompson had been at Glacier Lodge and overheard Clyde talking about his "old wreck of a car" that he could not depend on to make the trip to Bishop for a dental appointment. He was relegated to bumming rides to get to his appointments, as well as to replenish his supplies in Big Pine and Bishop. Thompson said in her letter that she thought it was sad that Clyde was unaware of the admiration that people held for him, and she suggested that the members of the Sierra Club "would want to show him in a tangible way what they really did think of him by getting him a sturdy car of some kind that he could keep his cameras and mountain equipment in, that would make his life up there in the mountains more easy for him." Jackson forwarded the letter to Sierra Club Secretary Charlotte Mauk, who in turn circulated it to the club's board of directors for comment. Richard Leonard weighed in first with a terse "no chance." Lewis Clark, Einar Nilsson, and David Brower followed suit. Mauk responded to Jackson: "As you may realize Norman is no longer young, and may, through exaggeration, give the impression he is not appreciated. He'd had a couple of battles with Oliver [Kehrlein] which left him (NC) rather embittered, I believe. It's too bad."[19]

In her formal response to Thompson, Mauk wrote that her letter had been "circulated to several of our officers, but their discussions have turned up no workable suggestions, and we do not know of any means of meeting such a problem as you pose." Mauk went on to tell Jackson:

It may, however, comfort you to know that members of the 1941 High Trip (before things got quite so difficult as they now are!) *did* express their appreciation to Norman in a material way. When he let it be known that this was the last year in which he expected to accompany the trip, a sizeable purse was raised by cash contributions and pledges and by contributions of artists' work for auction. (I happen to know that some people, who had known and enjoyed Norman during many trips, made larger contributions than they could really afford.) Of course that was a long time ago, and money is scarcer now—which makes Norman's as well as other people's problems more acute. As one to whom

Norman had shown many kindnesses, I wish with you that something could be done.[20]

Fortunately, Norman's conflicts with the Sierra Club leadership
didn't keep him from enjoying accolades from the rank-and-file. He
attended numerous banquets and gatherings at which he was both a
speaker and a guest of honor. These included the 1946 Southern California Chapter's annual dinner, and the seventy-fifth jubilee, in 1967.
According to Southern California Chapter leader Richard Searle, "I
remember, at that banquet, he [Norman] started talking and they
had a hard time stopping him."[21] In 1970 the first Francis Farquhar
Mountaineering Award was presented jointly to Norman Clyde and
Allen Steck, for their contributions to the field of mountaineering
and to the Sierra Club's prestige in this field.[22] This award from the
Sierra Club is particularly significant: it cames from an organization
that first embraced, then rejected, and finally accepted a person more
rugged and individualistic than most of the club's bohemian membership. Despite the strained relationship, however, Clyde continued to
accompany Sierra Club outings into the mountains throughout the
1950s and '60s. Smoke Blanchard referred to his friend on these trips
as "'King of the woodpile,' general storyteller and a sort of museum
exhibition, being, as Clyde said, 'about 900 years old.'"[23]

Michael Cohen, author of a history of the Sierra Club, while agree-
ing that Norman Clyde was an "essential ingredient" of Sierra Club
excursions, also acknowledged that Clyde's stubborn independence
could cast a shadow over an outing. In his *History of the Sierra Club,
1892–1970* he writes about the time Clyde was a companion on an
outing that Cohen had organized in 1968. Cohen was reading a selection penned by John Muir entitled "Snow Banners of the California
Alps"[24] and when Cohen had finished, "Norman Clyde stood up and
kicked the fire. 'Muir was no real mountaineer. He spent all his time
down in Yosemite Valley.' His eyes burned in their sockets; his set teeth
gleamed in the firelight above his grizzled jaw. The silence of the forty
campers lasted until the old gaffer had passed into the dark toward his
sleeping place."[25]

Surprisingly, "Snow Banners" is one of the chapters in Muir's *The
Mountains of California*, which is the same work that had inspired
Clyde to come to the Golden State in 1910 and join the Sierra Club
four years later. It might have been that the anger Clyde seemed to
harbor toward Muir was actually directed at the Sierra Club, both for

its members' continued veneration of Muir and also for the treatment he had received at the hands of some of the club's elite. Even at the age of eighty-three, Clyde was sensitive to any real or perceived slight. His receipt of the Farquhar Mountaineering Award probably went a long way to easing his ill feelings toward some of the club members, and the organization in general.[26]

In yet another odd twist on the Muir/Clyde issue is this perspective from his friend Thomas Jukes: "The mantle of John Muir—not Muir, the leader, but Muir, the devotee of the mountains of California—descended to Norman Clyde, who dropped out of society in the 1920s to lead a solitary, hippie (but non-drug) life in the southern Sierra Nevada. The older leaders of the club regard Norman Clyde as a Dalai Lama."[27] This bit of prose was written in a private letter, and it is probably a good thing that Clyde was not privy to its content, as he most assuredly would have taken exception to his characterization as a "hippie" and the Dalai Lama. If the mantle of "devotee of the mountains of California" had indeed passed from Muir to Clyde, its passage surely went unnoticed by most of the state's population, as Clyde was known to only a relative handful of the state's inhabitants.

"My Own Private Concern"[28]

There were three things in Clyde's life that he was reluctant to talk about: women, religion, and politics. He was a reserved and decorous man, and his very private nature kept his opinions on such matters silenced. Also, perhaps there was a simple lack of interest in Clyde about matters of the heart, the soul, and the world at large.

Norman's friend Smoke Blanchard states that Clyde had only infrequent and casual contacts with women, but that does not seem to be the case. He regularly stayed in touch with his sisters and his mother, and he carried out correspondence with other female friends. He did not consciously avoid or shun women as a group, and his support of female climbers clearly shows he was not a misogynist.

Dorothy Pepper recalled in a 1976 interview that she met Norman Clyde on her first Sierra Club outing to Yellowstone in 1926. She knew about him because her friend Julie had climbed with him and typed up many of his articles for publication. On his occasional forays into Los Angeles Clyde would visit Dorothy and her friends, bringing along his scrapbook filled with photographs of mountains. "When he came to see us, he would sit down, open up his book and say, 'This is Mt. Whitney looking south. This is Mt. Whitney looking south by southeast. This is Mt. Whitney looking...' I think he took a picture from every one of the three hundred sixty-five degrees [sic]. There were just piles of them. One night Alice Carter and I couldn't stand it anymore. We thought we would get rid of him; otherwise he'd stay until one in the morning. So we got a bunch of alarm clocks, set them and hid them all around in furniture. Julie didn't know this. When the first one went off, she went to the telephone and said, 'Hello, Hello.' Nothing happened. Then she went back and another one went off and it never fazed him at all. One night he came to the house with two neckties on...He had one the right way, another one way under his ear."[29] Norman may have been narrowly focused in his interests, but when he found others—men or women—who shared his enthusiasms, he enjoyed their company and camaraderie.

He did not, however, get along so well with the women who supplied him his winter quarters. (In exchange for keeping the roofs free of snow and watching over the property during the long, quiet winter months, Clyde was given a place to stay, rent-free.) His first twenty winters in the Sierra were spent at Glacier Lodge, courtesy of Bertha Horine, and by all accounts their relationship was a rocky one. His last twenty years were spent at Baker Ranch, above Big Pine. Old habits die hard, and his conflicts with the owner were similar to those with Horine.

Nevertheless, it is unlikely that Clyde's difficult relations with his winter landlords was due to their gender. There is plenty of evidence that he got along with, if not all women, at least those who could climb well. The renowned botanist Mary DeDecker and her husband, Paul, spent many weekends and vacations hiking in the Sierra Nevada with their two daughters, and they often met Clyde in the backcountry, often sharing evening campfires together. Mary remembers that townspeople often said that Clyde "didn't have any use for women, but he admired our daughters, who were pretty good mountaineers in their own right."[30] Furthering the notion that Clyde got along with women who shared his interest in the outdoors, bookman Glen Dawson recalls that Clyde would come to Los Angeles once or twice a year to participate in Sierra Club activities and he was a "good friend" of two Sierra Club members there, Lina Pierce and Dorothy Willard.[31]

Clyde's relationships with women did not change as he grew older. Cecelia Hurwich was on a Sierra Club wilderness outing in the summer of 1969 when she met Norman. He walked into their base camp with a sixty-five-pound pack on his back and later that evening set up Hurwich's tube tent during a storm. According to Hurwich, all of the women in the group found him charming, and he himself had a twinkle in his eye for the ladies, even though he was in his eighties.[32] Mary DeDecker recalled a field trip to the White Mountains east of Owens Valley when Clyde's health was faltering. He had taken his huge bedroll up slope away from the group and, because Mary was concerned for him, she checked in on him before turning in herself. She says she recalls thinking, "'What is this woman doing checking on an old mountaineer?' But I think he liked it."[33]

If little can be said about Norman's feelings toward women, much less can be said of his outlook on religion and politics. Perhaps it was his upbringing in a Christian household, and his matriculation in a Christian college, but Clyde never seemed to participate in organized religion, especially after the death of his wife. In a 1963 interview with an unidentified reporter from the *Los Angeles Times*, Clyde said of his dismissal from his job as principal of Independence High School in 1928, "I didn't see eye-to-eye with the powers to be [sic]. The old ladies said teachers should go to church every Sunday. Well, I didn't have anything against churches, but I never got around to going."[34] The only other account we have of these subjects is from Smoke Blanchard. Smoke recalled that Norman would make jokes about "going to the hot place" (i.e., hell), but beyond that, his friend never showed any interest in religious or philosophical matters. Smoke went on to say that "now and then he muttered about the latest political news. He seemed to be mildly liberal, or at least somewhat antiwar and antiaggression, but I doubt if he bothered to think of such things much."[35] For a man who lived through two world wars, as well as the Spanish American War, the Korean War, and Vietnam, he may well have had his fill of global conflict. As a classical scholar, he also knew of the tragedy, futility, and wastefulness of such endeavors, and perhaps preferred instead to turn his eyes and his mind toward the beauty of the world.

CHAPTER 10

Between the Pioneers and the Rock Climbers: Norman Clyde's Legacy

Despite old age and physical infirmity, Norman Clyde led a full and rich life right up to the end. Walt Wheelock observed that Clyde had mellowed somewhat in his later years, a shift in outlook and attitude that Smoke Blanchard and others also noted. There was always something or someone to complain about, and sometimes it was even justified, however, the Old Gaffer also seemed to be learning to take things in stride, and his once famous and ferocious temper subsided with the passing years.

Perhaps one reason for the shift was the series of losses Clyde suffered in the 1950s and '60s. His brother Arthur passed away in 1954 of acute appendicitis while on a fishing trip in Canada; his sister Clara died in 1957 at the age of sixty-eight. Clyde's own mortality may have been weighing on his mind, as he made more frequent trips home and encouraged his family to visit him in California. Travel for him was difficult; he lacked the resources to go by plane or train and had to take the bus back to Pennsylvania, a long and uncomfortable trip.

He made periodic visits to his family in the Midwest, once on the occasion of his receipt of the Distinguished Service Award from Geneva College in 1962. The family traveled together to a Michigan cabin they owned, and Clyde went along. His niece Vida Brown recalls that he could identify which rocks were the oldest in the area, and that he always was adept at searching out and finding the most beautiful place to sit and enjoy the scenery. The Reverend James Carson and his wife accompanied the Clydes to their cabin, and he remembers Norman taking his (Norman's) sister Sarah to task for squandering kindling. Reverend Carson recalls that Clyde "used such material sparingly to light his fires in the mountains. His survival instincts and training were very much alive."[1]

It was well known that Clyde relied on his abilities, skills, instincts, and many years of experience to survive and thrive under difficult circumstances, but he had also amassed a large cache of material that aided him in his day-to-day endeavors: guns, fishing equipment, and assorted mountaineering gear, all of which was stashed in the cabin at Glacier Lodge, and later at Baker Ranch. Hooligans from Owens Valley were well aware of Clyde's collections, and as early as 1950 he was writing to his friend Jules Eichorn complaining about Glacier Lodge: "This place appears to be a veritable den of thieves. To date I have lost some $150.00 worth of equipment stolen by [illegible] lodge people or [illegible] and it is getting pretty bad when they even steal my boots."[2] The theme recurs a decade later, when Clyde writes to Jules that he "had to stay around during the quail hunting season, particularly during the weekends to be sure that none of my windows should not be shot out. There wasn't much that I could do except see that they did not shoot within the 150 yard line [of the house] (state law). Since the close of the season very few have been around. The local hoodlums also appear to give the place a wide berth, since at least one of their number, a high school boy, had the pleasure of spending a few weekends in jail—just to give him a little time to ponder over his ways."[3]

Clyde's fondness for firearms never left him. He always enjoyed collecting, carrying, and shooting guns, a legacy of his early years in the Pennsylvania and Canadian woods. He maintained an "artillery proving ground" for "exercising" his rifles and handguns on a regular basis, and he was a member of the National Rifle Association.

Along with climbing, skiing, fishing, and hiking, Clyde maintained an equal interest in and passion for photography. He secured views of the mountain peaks and passes that few others had seen, and his photographs frequently accompanied the articles he wrote for publication.[4]

Then, as if Clyde didn't already have enough hobbies, he took up gardening in his final years. He would haul wheelbarrow loads of manure from an old stable on the ranch and work it into the soil. Using water from Baker Creek he would irrigate the flowers he planted, guarding them from foraging cows.

Clyde remained an energetic man who needed to be productive. He expressed himself in a letter to Jules, "I should do considerable writing, but what with a [sic] 101 hobbies to occupy my time, chronic lethargy, and difficulty in [illegible] I do very little [illegible]. I do considerable reading—perhaps too much, and in a sort of variety—foreign languages, science—chiefly geology and biology, adventure and the devil only knows what."[5]

As Clyde became more sedentary with age, he could also be social, entertaining (in his own way) friends and admirers who came to call on the Old Gaffer. Clyde had a young visitor for his eightieth birthday, in 1965. Robert Sydnor was a John Muir High School student in Pasadena who was an outdoor enthusiast that had read *Close Ups of the High Sierra* and had purposely sought out its now elderly author. Sydnor made his way to Baker Ranch in his Jeep plastered with "John Muir High School" stickers, a sight Clyde regarded with quiet amusement. The young man stayed for several days, camping out a respectable distance from his host, whom he noted was also "sleeping outdoors on an ancient mattress that was elevated two feet off the ground on some kind of cot." Sydnor interviewed Clyde at length and took several pictures of him. Clyde invited Sydnor to return any time and was "quite astonished" that anyone would travel such a long distance to wish him a happy birthday.[6]

The Long Decline and the Final Climb

After having lived a remarkably healthy life, his years of mountain dwelling began to take their toll. When Clyde returned home to Pennsylvania in 1962 to receive his award from Geneva College he was suffering from mastoid infection in his ear, a painful condition that made it difficult for him to be at high elevations. Clyde's niece Vida Brown believes this chronic condition may have contributed to her uncle's death. Walt Wheelock thought that Clyde had suffered from an enlarged heart for several years, possibly as a result of his having lived so long in thin air.[7] In 1969 Clyde had his cancerous left eye removed in an operation at Cottage Hospital in Santa Barbara, although it is likely the disease was genetic rather than an affliction brought on by environmental conditions. On April 25, 1969, Norman wrote to Dr. James W. Rowe at Cottage Hospital:

The eye appears to be doing very well—at least there are no symptoms to the contrary. As the Inyo County Sanitarium [sic] is within a mile of the old Ranch house, which has been my head-quarters for eight or ten years, I drive over there every morning to have the eye checked on and the dressing changed. Upon my return here I was obliged to do considerable road construction to get in and out in my car; and have to do some hydraulic engi-neering diverting an overflow from Baker Creek back into the main channel. There has been and still is considerable swamp-ing out of fallen trees and branches, which I call bushwhack-ing. Although these are not presently the sort of activities that a person just released from a hospital should indulge in, I do not seem to have suffered any ill effects from them. You might tell Dr. Crowder that the "eye" appears to be doing exceptionally well and that Dr. Hough may report to him regarding the condition of the eye before my return to the hospital several weeks hence. Thanks for the very considerate and efficient service, which I received at your hospital. Very Truly, Norman Clyde.[8]

Unfortunately, by the time Clyde's cancer was diagnosed and his eye removed, the cancer may have already spread.

His sister Sarah and her husband, Henry McKelvey, came to Cali-fornia to check on their brother. It was Sarah who had arranged for Clyde's treatment at Cottage Hospital. While he was recuperating they were able to spend some time with him and tour the Sierra Nevada, with Clyde showing them some of his favorite places, including Kings Canyon.[9] Later that summer Clyde was already back in the moun-tains, at a Sierra Club campout. A friend in Big Pine reported to Mrs. McKelvey that Norman "seems fine—looks better than I have seen him for some time....I have been watching his place since he's been away [at base camp]."[10] Clyde's last camp was at 10,000 feet, in the Fourth Recess of Mono Creek. In the summer of 1970, at the age of eighty-five, he made the final trek on foot, over the crest of the Sierra, his last mountain outing.[11]

One of Clyde's final indignities occurred when he entered the Inyo County Sanatorium for a hernia operation. While he was convalescing, vandals broke into his Baker Ranch house and ransacked it, stealing some items of no use to anyone else but Clyde. Perhaps in search of his weapons cache, they cleaned him out of his kitchenware, the kero-sene lamps that he used to read by, even his tools. They trashed his extensive collection of manuscripts and photographs, throwing them around as if they were only so much useless paper. This was the scene that greeted Clyde, Jules Eichorn, and Smoke Blanchard when they returned to the cabin on Baker Creek. Taking stock of the destruction, Norman quietly sat down on the ground and began organizing his papers and photographs into neat piles. When the lifetime of work was separated, sorted, and collected, the trio left. After that, Clyde was unable to move back to the cabin and spent the rest of his days in the sanatorium. Robert Sydnor and his father visited Clyde there for a few hours and found him reading books in Latin, Greek, and Italian. Clyde commented that he regretted not having the thousands of books that he had collected over a lifetime, as the sanatorium limited his collection to only about a hundred books.[12]

Two years later, Norman Asa Clyde died on December 23, 1972, at 12:45 in the morning. He was eighty-seven years old.[13] The cause of death as stated in his death certificate reads, "metastatic melanoma—primary in eye." His body was taken to the Grandview Crematorium in Glendale; according to the certificate, he was inurned in the Tonopah Cemetery in Nevada. But such an ignominious end did not seem proper for a man who spent more than sixty years living in the mountains, and a gathering of Clyde's friends transported his remains to the top of Norman Clyde Peak, at the headwaters of the South and Middle Forks of Big Pine Creek. The "funeral party" consisted of Smoke Blanchard, Bob Blanchard, Jules Eichorn, and Nort Benner. Eichorn's son Peter and Blanchard's wife, Su, operated the funeral base camp at Finger Lake. The party picked its way along a series of ledges above the North Clyde Glacier, carefully hauling the special cargo in a rucksack. Once on top of the narrow summit, the group took turns hurling handfuls of the human ash that had been their powerful friend. The ashes drifted over the northeast face, where the wind carried them out onto the glaciers and into the cracks of the rock that Clyde had once trod. When the cardboard container was empty, the group slowly picked its way back down the mountain, one man missing from the entourage but present, then as always, in spirit.[14]

Walt Wheelock wrote a fine death notice for Clyde that appeared in the February 1973 edition of the *Southern Sierran*, the newsletter of the Angeles Chapter of the Sierra Club. Clyde's passing, however, was not mentioned in the *Sierra Club Bulletin*, perhaps an indication of the growth of the organization and its emphasis on environmental issues around the nation and the world. Thomas Jukes, a Sierra Club member, climber, and noted molecular biologist, penned an obituary that appeared in the *American Alpine Journal*, writing that Clyde "had lived as every alpinist wants to live, but as none of them dare to do, and so he had a unique life. When he died, I felt that an endangered species had become extinct....He was the only man I know who gave himself up completely to a passionate love of the mountains. In return, the mountains spared him a hundred times as he clambered alone to their summits by many a new route, and they let him die of old age, in full view of their peaks."[15] A death notice also appeared in *Summit* magazine for January–February 1973, accompanied by a caricature sketch of Clyde by Bishop artist and sign painter Sheridan Anderson. The cartoon drew an angry response from Mr. and Mrs. Tom Ross of Independence, who wrote to the magazine, "We think it is ludicrous to depict Mr. Clyde in this fashion, as a fat man with a stupid look on his face and a patch on his pants and flower on his hat. It is insulting to his friends to see such a cartoon of a wonderful man who is now dead. His love for the mountains was serious, not something to be laughed at."[16] When *Summit*'s "Award Winning 1974 Sheridan Anderson Abominable Mountaineering Calendar" appeared, there was a full page devoted to Clyde, with a new handsome pen-and-ink portrait of Norman. In the accompanying text, Jules Eichorn wrote,

It is sometimes difficult for me to believe that Norman Clyde is no longer a part of the Sierra Nevada. He was around for what seemed an eternity and when a man of Clyde's stature departs, a boundless void can be felt by those that intimately knew him. Our association spanned some forty plus years. In that time I got to know the man under a variety of conditions—some pretty wild but none in which Clyde was not in complete control of whatever situation that was. If it was a difficult route, his "sixth sense" told him what he could or could not do. Once he made the climb, he seemed never to forget the route. Time and again in his later years we would talk about a climb and his recall of each detail was absolute. He was that way in all that he did. In a sense he was a perfectionist....I could continue about Clyde's knowledge and abilities concerning so many things: mountain sheep and other fauna; his botanical knowledge; his selection of a "boudoir"[;] but it really isn't necessary. Suffice to say that he lived closer to the mountains than any other man I knew. It was as if an osmotic effect was taking place: the mountains breathing life into Norman and he reciprocating. Above all, it was the absolute integrity of the man that seemed to be the key to Clyde's greatness. Whether it was climbing a peak, noting a geological phenomenon, or taking a picture—that particular trait stood out. He put it all together.[17]

Norman Clyde and His Place in History

One goal of this biography has been to place Norman Clyde into historical context. His life and accomplishments were shaped, in part, by people and events that preceded him. Clyde, in turn, was affected by, and had an effect on, his own era, as well as his contemporaries. The brief discussion that follows is an attempt to place this rugged individual within the context of his time and chosen location, and against the backdrop of history, so that his achievements might be better understood and appreciated.

Clyde's relationship to California's natural world invokes comparisons with early explorers Jedediah Smith, Joseph Walker, and John C. Fremont, along with the transcendental John Muir and the brooding and brilliant poet Robinson Jeffers. But Clyde, although similar to his forebears, remained unique. Whereas in his extended forays into the mountains Clyde took special note of the presence of Native American predecessors in the high country—the occasional obsidian scatter or flaked stone tool would catch his eye and remind him that he wasn't the first person to come this way—the explorers Smith, Walker, and Fremont were just passing through, on their way to someplace else. For them the mountains were an obstacle to be surmounted, not a destination for exploration. Clyde, on the other hand, lived in them for nearly sixty years.

John Muir died at the age of seventy-six in 1914, the same year Clyde became a member of the Sierra Club. Muir was an energetic explorer and defender of the Range of Light who was also possessed of a bright and sparkling personality and a gregarious manner. With his lyrical and descriptive writings, he endeared himself to thousands of mountain aficionados during his life and to countless explorers and armchair enthusiasts after his death. Muir was also a pragmatist who married into a monied family, operated a successful farm, and strode the halls of the state capitol and Congress in defense of his beloved Yosemite and the Sierra Nevada. For someone like Clyde, however, such a life involved too many compromises and too little time spent outdoors, tradeoffs he couldn't bring himself to bear.

There were other Sierra Club members with whom Clyde associated that went on to successful careers in publishing, teaching, the law, real estate, and accounting. They took active roles in the management and administration of the Sierra Club, and became embroiled in some of its most difficult and contentious environmental battles of the twentieth century. David Brower, Richard Leonard, and Francis Farquhar are just a few of the Sierra Club luminaries whose lives were lived in the urban centers and whose *vacations* were spent in the high country. Clyde was not of their ilk, nor they of his. While these Brahmins held Clyde in some esteem for his climbing prowess, it cannot be readily stated that Clyde returned the compliment regarding their chosen fields.

Robinson Jeffers figures in this discussion as well, not as someone who was associated with Clyde but as an individual who shared many of the reclusive mountaineer's traits. Jeffers's chosen place of refuge was on Carmel Bay, to which he moved in 1914 and where for many years he could avoid the crowds and conditions of other parts of the state while he wrote his powerful narrative poetry. Jeffers's nature writings have found favor among environmentalists, some of whom have embraced Jeffers's philosophy of "inhumanism," that is, a perspective placing humans into what is regarded as their rightful place in the universe. It is an outlook and philosophy that Clyde would have appreciated, as he deeply revered the natural world and kept himself at some distance from human events and activities that he deemed unworthy of his time or energy. Jeffers's writings enjoyed a resurgence of popularity following the poet's death in 1962, and his work was republished by the Sierra Club and others and used to great effort to further define and describe the "deep ecology" movement.

Similarly, Clyde came into favor once again toward the end of his life with a younger generation, one that did not know of his earlier tempestuous days but that admired him for his climbing feats, daring rescues and body recoveries, and his chosen lifestyle. They saw in him someone who believed in what he stood for, defended what he believed to be true, and lived his life according to his own code of standards and conduct. It is in this way that Clyde most resembles the ideal set forth in Ralph Waldo Emerson's essay on self-reliance.

The passage of time is a necessary requirement in order to accurately gauge a person's contribution to history. In Norman Clyde's case, the years like storm clouds have alternately obscured and revealed his unique position in mountaineering annals. A critical appraisal of his life confirms his place in the pantheon of explorers, guides, and writers who made worthwhile and lasting contributions to our understanding and appreciation of the natural world.

Conclusion

Throughout this work the words of Norman Clyde have been used to tell the story of his life and times. In addition, the writings, correspondence, and recollections of Clyde's family, friends, fellow climbers, and acquaintances further illuminate and offer insight into this fascinating and complex person. How much can (or should) one know about a mountain man who savored his solitude?

The question also remains, why should Clyde be remembered, not only by the climbing community that he helped perpetuate but by anyone who is interested in the history of the Sierra Nevada, California, and western North America in general? Clyde's combination into one man of rugged outdoorsman, intellectual scholar, social misfit and, ultimately, a touchstone for a new generation makes him a unique person in the state's history and landscape.

Clyde explored the vertical world of the High Sierra entirely under his own power. In his own words, he came "between the pioneers and the real rock climbers." He was the first person to ascend more than two hundred peaks throughout western North America, climbing more than one thousand peaks in his lifetime. Without his example, far fewer people would have ventured into the wilderness to see what he had seen and described to them in numerous articles. Clyde had a great impact, not only on contemporary and future climbers but also on the popularity of mountain travel and increasing general knowledge of the High Sierra.

Clyde didn't just visit the mountains, he lived in them. He not only climbed the high peaks, he explored the deep canyons in search of pristine fish-filled pools. He searched for quiet shelters among the boulders and foxtail pines, where he could read, drowse, and gaze upon snow-covered mountains and flower-carpeted meadows. He snowshoed in winter, skied in spring, hiked and climbed throughout summer and fall.

Clyde's world was elemental: granite and glacial ice, green mountain meadows and deep blue sky. He was often alone in this rugged and austere world with only his private thoughts, observations, and memories to keep him company. Today, if you are in the vicinity of the Palisades, the Minarets, or Mt. Whitney; at Glacier Lodge in Yosemite or Giant Forest in Sequoia; scrambling up an alpine peak or ambling down a river canyon, drink in your surroundings, and think of Norman Clyde.

TIMELINE

1885 .... Norman Asa Clyde is born on April 8 in Philadelphia.

1890 .... Yosemite, Sequoia, and General Grant National Parks are created.

1892 .... Sierra Club is founded and John Muir is elected its president.

1894 .... John Muir's collection of essays *The Mountains of California* is published.

1895 .... Theodore S. Solomons and Walter A. Starr, Sr., pioneer a high mountain route between Yosemite and Kings Canyon.

1901 .... Charles Clyde dies of pneumonia at the age of forty-six, leaving Norman as the oldest of nine children in the Clyde household. The first Sierra Club outing is organized by John Muir and led by William E. Colby.

1909 .... Clyde graduates from Geneva College in Beaver Falls, Pennsylvania, and heads west.

1910 .... Clyde is in California, exploring the Sierra Nevada from Sequoia to Yosemite and the Mt. Shasta region. Glacier National Park is established.

1913 .... The Raker Act grants the City and County of San Francisco the right to dam Hetch Hetchy Valley in Yosemite National Park.

1914 .... Clyde makes first ascents of Electra Peak, Mt. Parker, and Foerster Peak. John Muir dies on December 24.

1915 .... Norman Clyde and Winifred May Bolster are married in Pasadena on June 15.

1916 .... Clyde's first climb of Mt. Shasta. The National Park Service Organic Act is signed into law.

1917 .... Clyde climbs Mt. San Jacinto with fellow Sierra Club members.

1919 .... Winifred May Bolster Clyde dies of tuberculosis on February 14. Clyde heads for the High Sierra, where he climbs Mt. Whitney twice, along with Mt. Brewer, East Vidette, Mt. Tyndall, Mt. Ritter, Electra Peak, and University Peak.

1920 .... Clyde makes first ascents of Mt. Huxley and Triple Divide Peak.

1922 .... George Mallory and Theodore Somervell climb to 8,230 meters (27,000 feet) on Mt. Everest without the use of bottled oxygen, setting a new high-altitude record.

1923 .... Clyde sets a new speed record for ascending Mt. Shasta. He goes on to Glacier National Park, where he climbs thirty-six peaks in thirty-six days, eleven of which are thought to be first ascents.

1924 .... George Mallory and Andrew Irvine disappear while climbing Mt. Everest; their remains would not be discovered until 1999. Clyde climbs another nineteen peaks in Glacier National Park in the summer of 1924, including a first ascent of Mt. Merritt. That fall he assumes the post of principal of Independence High School in Owens Valley.

1925 .... Clyde makes fifty-three climbs, including twenty-three first ascents in the Sierra Nevada.

1926 .... Clyde leads two Sierra Club parties up the Grand Teton in Wyoming and goes on to solo Mt. Moran. He climbs in Montana and Idaho before returning to Owens Valley. He also makes two first ascents of Mt. Russell in the Sierra in one day (June 24).

1927 .... Clyde climbs Mt. Whitney three times for a career total (to that date) of nine. He pioneers a new route on Mt. Agassiz and one on Table Mountain, in the Great Western Divide, with a young Glen Dawson. According to Steve Roper, Clyde climbs Independence Peak, south of Onion Valley in the Kearsarge Pass region, five times in 1926–27. According to *Touring Topics* editor Phil Townsend Hanna, by 1927 Clyde had climbed almost four hundred peaks in the West; Hanna calls Clyde "America's most irrepressible mountaineer."

1928 .... Clyde's series of articles, "'Close Ups' of Our High Sierra," appears in *Touring Topics*, the magazine of the Automobile Club of Southern California. Clyde makes a first ascent of the Minaret that would later bear his name. The Inyo County Board of Education accepts Clyde's resignation from the principalship of Independence High School.

1929 .... The United States stock market crashes.

1930 .... Clyde locates the body of fifteen-year-old Howard Lamel, who died while attempting to climb the east face of Mt. Whitney. Clyde has been performing rescues and recovering bodies in the Sierra for almost ten years.

1931 .... Robert L. M. Underhill and Francis Farquhar introduce the techniques of roped climbing and belays to climbers in Yosemite Valley. Later Underhill, along with Clyde, Glen Dawson, and Jules Eichorn, pioneer first ascents on the North Palisade, Thunderbolt Peak, and the east face of Mt. Whitney.

1932 .... Clyde leads a first ascent of El Picacho del Diablo in Baja California.

1933 .... Clyde discovers the remains of Walter A. Starr, Jr., on Michael Minaret following a month-long search by dozens of government workers and volunteers.

1934 .... *Starr's Guide to the John Muir Trail and the High Sierra Region*, by Walter A. Starr, Jr., is published by the Sierra Club. Jules Eichorn, Richard M. Leonard, and Bestor Robinson make the first ascent of the Higher and Lower Cathedral Spires in Yosemite Valley, utilizing pitons for the first time in the Sierra Nevada. In the summer Clyde discovers the remains of Mr. and Mrs. Conrad Rettenbacher, who died while climbing Banner Peak.

1935 .... William Dulley, a skiing partner of Clyde's, perishes during a spring snowstorm.

1937 .... Clyde returns to Baja California for his second ascent of El Picacho del Diablo, this time with *Desert Magazine* editor Randall Henderson.

1938 .... Clyde makes the first winter ascent of Mt. Winchell with David Brower and Morgan Harris.

1939 .... Clyde makes first ascents of new routes up Goodale Mountain and Deerhorn Mountain and down Mt. Stanford. Geneva College awards Clyde with an honorary Doctor of Science degree.

1940 .... Kings Canyon National Park is created. Clyde pioneers the glacier route on Mt. Gardiner.

1941 .... Clyde is fired by the Sierra Club as a High Trip leader. America enters World War II. An Army Air Corps plane crashes on Birch Mountain; Clyde leads the recovery effort in 1942.

1942 .... During the war years Clyde sustains himself by working for the U.S. Geological Survey.

1943 .... Harlow Russ and Herschel Asbury are critically injured on a climb of North Palisade; Clyde initiates and directs the rescue effort, saving both men's lives in what is considered the greatest rescue in American mountaineering to that time.

1946 .... Along with Jules Eichorn and others, Clyde pioneers new routes on Mt. Ericsson and Deerhorn Mountain. Clyde attends the annual banquet of the Southern California chapter of the Sierra Club. Lost Arrow Spire is climbed by Jack Arnold and Axel Nelson.

1950 .... Allen Steck and John Salathe climb Yosemite's first "big wall," the north face of Sentinel Rock. On June 3, Maurice Herzog and Louis Lachenal climb Annapurna, the first 8,000-meter (26,000-foot) peak to be summited.

1953 .... Edmund Hillary and Tensing Norgay are the first to reach the summit of Mt. Everest, while Hermann Buhl solo summits Nanga Parbat, both in the Himalayas.

1954 .... K2, the second highest peak in the world, is climbed by
Italians Lino Lacedelli and Achille Compagnoni on July 31.

1958 .... The South Buttress of El Capitan is climbed by Warren
Harding, George Whitmore, and Wayne Merry.

1962 .... Geneva College presents Norman Asa Clyde with a
Distinguished Service Award for his nature writings. Walt
Wheelock publishes *Close Ups of the High Sierra*, a collection of
Clyde's writing.

1969 .... Neil Armstrong is the first man to walk on the moon.

1970 .... Along with Allen Steck, Clyde is presented with the first
Francis Farquhar Mountaineering Award from the Sierra
Club, for his contributions to the field of mountaineering
and to the Sierra Club's prestige in the field. He accompanies
his last Sierra Club trip at the age of eighty-five. Steve Roper
estimates Clyde made over one thousand ascents in the
Sierra Nevada, and that Clyde's first ascents and first routes
numbered more than one hundred and thirty.

1971 .... Scrimshaw Press of San Francisco publishes *Norman Clyde:
Rambles Through the Range of Light*.

1972 .... Norman Asa Clyde dies on December 23 in Big Pine,
California, at the age of eighty-seven.

1973 and
1974 .... The U.S. Board on Geographic Names bestows Clyde's name
on a prominent peak and glacier in the Palisade Range of the
Sierra Nevada, completing the recommendation that Hervey
Voge made in 1939.

END NOTES

INTRODUCTION

1. Norman Clyde, as quoted in "Grizzled Mountaineer 'On Top of the World,'" *Los Angeles Times,* September 22, 1963, H7.

2. Excerpted from "Clyde, Norman Asa," in *Who's Who in America* 34 (Chicago: Marquis Who's Who, 1967), 404.

CHAPTER 1

1. Genealogical records compiled by Clara Clyde Tomkies, courtesy of Vida Brown. Clyde's middle name comes from his maternal uncle, Asa Purvis; the origin of Norman's first name is unknown.

2. Vida Brown, personal communication, July 9, 1998. Arthur H. Clyde was later inaugurated into the High School Hall of Fame in Columbus, Ohio.

3. I am grateful to Dr. David Carson, Professor Emeritus at Geneva College, for bringing these poems to my attention.

4. Norman Clyde, "A Winter Sunrise," *The Geneva Cabinet,* February 1907. The other poem, "The Mountain Brook," was published in the October 1906 issue of the *Cabinet.* It describes a stream flowing through the mountains to the ocean and, like "A Winter Sunrise," has no discernable human presence.

5. Norman Clyde, "College Recreation," *The Geneva Cabinet.*

6. William F. Kimes and Maymie B. Kimes, *John Muir: A Reading Bibliography* (Fresno: Panorama West Books, 1986), 54. The book was reprinted at least five times before 1910, when Clyde left on his westward adventure.

7. Cyclops [Norman Clyde], "Roughing It on the Great Lakes," *The Geneva Cabinet* 33, no. 3 (December 1909), 8–11. My thanks to Vida Brown for bringing this to my attention, to Dr. David Carson for duplicating the article for me, and to Jason Manville for our discussions regarding Cyclops.

8. The story of Clyde arriving in Florence, Arizona, to teach school with a Colt firearm, and his observation that "they must have thought I was a damned funny-looking schoolteacher," can be found in William E. Smith, "Norman Clyde: Last of the Mountain Men," *Fortnight*, June–July 1957, 16–18. The catalog of his teaching career is detailed in "Clyde, Norman Asa," in *Who's Who in America* (1967), 404.

9. "Clyde, Norman Asa," in *Who's Who in America* (1967), 404; Walt Wheelock, "Norman Clyde," in *Close Ups of the High Sierra*, by Norman Clyde (Glendale, CA: La Siesta Press, 1962), 73.

10. Postcard in the Norman A. Clyde Collection, courtesy of the Eastern California Museum, Independence, California.

11. Ibid.

12. Harv Galic of Stanford University posted the following on his website: "Weaverville is a small community in Northern California, less than fifty miles from Mt. Shasta. According to the School District minutes, found by Michael Slater, at the end of the 1922/23 school year, on June 8, 1923, 'the clerk was instructed to notify Mr. Norman Clyde that his contract had expired and his services would no longer be required.'" I am grateful to Dr. Galic for his diligence in maintaining his website, www.stanford.edu/~galic/rettenbacher/index.html.

13. According to Jean Cleghorn McEuen, "Mr. Clyde was a friend of my father [Arthur Cleghorn] and a fellow teacher at Lowell High School in San Francisco. I remember he had red hair and pale blue eyes; he brought his wife to our home in Berkeley for a brief visit. (I think her name was Winifred)....I was a bit afraid of Mr. Clyde and I was a young teen-ager. Mr. Clyde did not teach very long at Lowell." Jean Cleghorn McEuen, letter, October 4, 1993.

14. From Walt Wheelock's essay on Clyde in *Close Ups of the High Sierra*, by Norman Clyde (1962).

15. Clyde did attend the University of Southern California during 1926 for postgraduate studies in education. See "Clyde, Norman Asa," in *Who's Who in America* (1967), 404.

16. Norman and Winifred's marriage certificate is in the Norman A. Clyde Collection, courtesy of the Eastern California Museum, Independence, California; Winifred May Clyde's death certificate was obtained through the State of California, Department of Health Services, Sacramento. According to Dave Bohn, Clyde did write a straightforward, ten-line letter to his mother notifying her of Winifred's death. Clyde noted that all concerned had expected Winifred to live longer, and that she had fought hard to beat the disease. He further mentioned that there were bills to

pay, and that it would take him a while to recover. Dave Bohn, letter, May 16, 1997.

17. Walter R. Bolster, letter, August 30, 1997.

CHAPTER 2

1. The first summit registers were placed in 1894 by members of the Sierra Club, who wanted to create a record of mountain exploration. The cylindrical tubes were placed on Mt. Conness, Mt. Lyell, Mt. Dana, Muir Gorge, Mt. Tallac, and Mt. Whitney. By 1905 there were forty summits throughout the range with registers. William D. Engs, "The Saga of the Registers," typewritten manuscript, 11 pp., n.d. Courtesy of Robin Ingraham, Jr.

2. Norman Clyde, "A Half Century of Climbing," in *Close Ups of the High Sierra* (1962), 67.

3. Robin Ingraham, Jr., "Norman Clyde's List of First Ascents in the Sierra Nevada" and "Norman Clyde's Ascent List," courtesy of Robin Ingraham, Jr. According to Walt Wheelock, Clyde made a total of fifty ascents of Mt. Whitney during his lifetime.

4. Excerpted from Michael P. Cohen, *The History of the Sierra Club, 1892–1970* (San Francisco: Sierra Club Books, 1988), 9. "Render accessible" was later changed to "preserve."

5. Walt Wheelock, "Norman Clyde," in *Close Ups of the High Sierra*, by Norman Clyde (1962), 73–74.

6. John W. Robinson, letter, August 26, 1993.

7. Robin Ingraham, Jr., "Norman Clyde's List of First Ascents in the Sierra Nevada"; Hervey Voge, ed., *A Climber's Guide to the High Sierra*, rev. ed. 1965 (San Francisco: Sierra Club, 1954), 57.

8. Walt Wheelock, "Norman Clyde," in *Close Ups of the High Sierra*, by Norman Clyde (1962), 74.

9. Harold Gilliam, "Old Man of the Mountains," *San Francisco Sunday Chronicle* "This World" (August 13, 1961), 3. Robin Ingraham, Jr., credits David Brower with bestowing this title on Clyde; Robin Ingraham, "Norman Clyde," *Climbing* magazine (December 1988), 95–96.

10. Hervey Voge, ed. *A Climber's Guide to the High Sierra* (1954), 134.

11. Robin Ingraham, Jr., "Norman Clyde's List of First Ascents in the Sierra Nevada"; Hervey Voge, ed., *A Climber's Guide to the High Sierra* (1954), 205.

12. The following summer McCoy repeated his climb, this time summiting in two hours and thirty minutes. In 1925 the Sierra Club sponsored a race up Mt. Shasta: eighteen-year-old David Lawyer of Pasadena won the contest with a time of two hours and twenty-four minutes; McCoy came in second; Clyde declined to participate, as he was actively climbing in the Eastern Sierra, and he was not in favor of such outright displays of competition among climbers. A. F. Eichorn, Sr., *The Mount Shasta Story* (Mt. Shasta: *Mt. Shasta Herald,* 1957), 66–88.

13. Norman Clyde, "First Ascent of Mount Wilbur," *Sierra Club Bulletin* 12, no. 1 (1924), 2–6.

14. Press release courtesy of Jules and Shirley Eichorn.

15. Ibid.

16. Norman Clyde, "Ascent of Mount Merritt," *Sierra Club Bulletin* 12, no. 2 (1925), 165–167.

17. "Glacier Park Peak Scaled First Time. Four California Men, Sierra Club Members, Climb Mount Kinnerly," *Great Falls Tribune,* August 5, 1937.

CHAPTER 3

1. Leonard recalled that the incident occurred in "1930 or '31, maybe a little earlier." Richard M. Leonard, "Mountaineer, Lawyer, Environmentalist," Vol. 1, an interview conducted by Susan R. Schrepfer (Berkeley: the Bancroft Library Regional Oral History Office and the Sierra Club Oral History Series, 1975), 15–17; courtesy of the Regional Oral History Office, Bancroft Library, University of California Berkeley.

2. Norman Clyde, "My Colt Woodsman," undated manuscript, five pp. In the Norman Asa Clyde Collection, courtesy of the Bancroft Library, University of California, Berkeley.

3. Neill C. Wilson, "A Prodigious Climber of Mountains," *National Motorist* (April 1928), 11.

4. According to Omie Mairs, "for a grown man, we thought that was a little unusual." "Conversation between Omie Mairs and Mary Millman re: Halloween Incident and Norman Clyde, 1928," tape recorded interview, Independence, California, July 1974. In the Norman A. Clyde Collection, courtesy of the Eastern California Museum, Independence, California.

5. Ibid.

6. This assertion is repeated in the September 22, 1963, *Los Angeles Times* article "Grizzled Mountaineer 'On Top of the World,'" which reads, "Clyde fired a revolver into the air, according to his recollection, to turn some young pranksters from school property. Although no one was hurt he was discharged from his job."

7. "Principal Resigned," *Inyo Register*, November 8, 1928.

8. In a survey of his private correspondence over a forty-year period, Clyde frequently disparaged Owens Valley residents. See Dennis Kruska, *Twenty-Five Letters from Norman Clyde, 1923–1964* (Los Angeles: Dawson's Book Shop, 1998); Clyde to Katherine G. Connable, January 28, 1966, in the Norman A. Clyde Collection, Eastern California Museum, Independence, California.

CHAPTER 4

1. Glen Dawson, letter, June 23, 1993.

2. Norman B. Livermore, Jr., personal communication, April 19, 1996, Martinez, California.

3. Wendell W. Moyer writes, "This derogatory sobriquet no doubt allud[ed] to the fact that he was reputed to neither bathe or change his clothes with any regularity." "The Beekeeper of McElvoy Canyon," *Newsletter for Friends of the Eastern California Museum* 10, no. 2 (Spring 1994), 5.

4. Dorothy Pepper Leavitt, "High Trip High Jinks," an interview conducted by Terry Kirker, in *Southern Sierrans* (California State University, Fullerton, Oral History Program and the Sierra Club History Committee, 1976), 28.

5. Ibid.

6. William E. Smith, "Norman Clyde: Last of the Mountain Men," *Fortnight* (June–July 1957), 16–18.

7. Ibid.

8. Dorothy Pepper Leavitt, "High Trip High Jinks" (1976); Glen Dawson, "Pioneer Rock Climber and Ski Mountaineer," an interview conducted by Richard Searle, in *Sierra Club Reminiscences II*, Sierra Club Oral History Project (1975), 3–4, courtesy of the Regional Oral History Office, Bancroft Library, University of California, Berkeley.

9. Ernest Dawson, "Climbing the Grand Teton. I. The First Sierra Club Party," *Sierra Club Bulletin* 12, no. 4 (1927), 354–359.

10. Ibid.

11. Norman Clyde, "Mountaineering in the Rockies. I. Mount Moran, Wyoming," *Sierra Club Bulletin* 12, no. 4 (1927), 365–368.

12. Neill C. Wilson, "A Prodigious Climber of Mountains," *National Motorist* (April 1928), 11.

13. Neill C. Wilson, "Climbing the Grand Teton. II. Some History and a Holiday Romp," *Sierra Club Bulletin* 12, no. 4 (1927), 359–364.

14. Robin Ingraham, Jr., "Norman Clyde's List of First Ascents in the Sierra Nevada."

15. Norman Clyde, "Mountaineering in the Rockies. II. Granite Peak, Montana," *Sierra Club Bulletin* 12, no. 4 (1927), 368–372.

16. Robin Ingraham, Jr., "Norman Clyde's List of First Ascents in the Sierra Nevada."

17. Hervey Voge, *A Climber's Guide to the High Sierra* (rev. ed. 1965), 253.

18. Clipping authored by Phil Townsend Hanna from *Touring Topics*, November 1927, in the Norman Asa Clyde Collection, Bancroft Library, University of California, Berkeley.

19. Neill C. Wilson, "A Prodigious Climber of Mountains," *National Motorist* (April 1928).

20. Ibid.

21. Carl Sharsmith, letter, January 31, 1993.

22. Nelson P. Nies to the Eastern California Museum (letter), June 27, 1988.

23. As quoted in Elizabeth Stone O'Neill, *Mountain Sage: The Life Story of Carl Sharsmith, Yosemite's Famous Ranger/Naturalist* (Yosemite National Park: Yosemite Association, 1988), 90.

24. Norman Clyde, "'Close Ups' of Our High Sierra," *Touring Topics* (April 1928).

25. Ibid.

26. Norman Clyde, *Close Ups of the High Sierra* (1976), 32.

27. See Norman Clyde, "The First Ascent of the Highest of the Minarets [Clyde Minaret] Followed by a Traverse of Mt. Ritter from the South," in

Norman Clyde of the Sierra Nevada: Rambles Through the Range of Light by Norman Clyde (San Francisco: Scrimshaw Press, 1971).

28. Walter L. Huber, "The Sierra Club in the Land of the Athabaska," *Sierra Club Bulletin* 14, no. 1 (February 1929), 1–12.

29. Ibid. Huber wrote of the "two tall lithe strangers…[that] they are of the third generation of mountain guides in a family whose name, Fuhrer, means guide, and well do they bear it."

30. Barbara Bedayn, personal communication, September 13, 1993.

31. Bestor Robinson, "The Ascent of Mount Edith Cavell," *Sierra Club Bulletin* 14, no. 1 (February 1929), 20–21.

32. Ibid.

33. Walter L. Huber, "The Sierra Club in the Land of the Athabaska" (1929), 4.

34. Norman Clyde, "The Sierra Club Ascent of Mount Geikie," *Sierra Club Bulletin* 14, no. 1 (February 1929), 20–24.

35. Marion Montgomery, "Ascent of Mount Robson—1928," *Sierra Club Bulletin* 14, no. 1 (February 1929), 13–19.

36. Ibid., 17.

37. Ibid.

38. Lowell Whittemore, "Up Mount Whitehorn," *Sierra Club Bulletin* 14, no. 1 (February 1929), 25–27.

39. Walter L. Huber, "The Sierra Club in the Land of the Athabaska" (1929). Although Huber wasn't on this particular trip, he was part of the larger Sierra Club party that made the trip to Canada, and he wrote these words on the occasion of the group's last campfire before leaving for home.

40. Norman Clyde, "High-Low," *Touring Topics* (November 1930). I thank William Preston for securing this article for me.

41. Ibid.

42. Robert L. M. Underhill, "On the Use and Management of the Rope in Rock Work," *Sierra Club Bulletin* 16, no. 1 (February 1931), 67.

43. Jules Eichorn, "Prologue," in *Norman Clyde of the Sierra Nevada: Rambles Through the Range of Light,* by Norman Clyde (1971).

44. Notes of interview, courtesy of Jules and Shirley Eichorn.

45. Jules Eichorn, "Prologue," in *Norman Clyde of the Sierra Nevada: Rambles Through the Range of Light,* by Norman Clyde (1971).

46. Norman Clyde, "Up the East Face of Whitney," *Touring Topics* (December 1931), 35–37.

47. In the 1930s the Sierra Club devised a rating system for climbing, ranging from Class 1 (walking) to Class 5 (technical climbing requiring specialized equipment, in addition to great skill, strength, stamina, and agility). The use of ropes and belaying techniques for personal protection are mandatory for most people climbing at the Class 4 and 5 levels. A "pitch" is the distance one can safely climb while on belay.

48. Dave Bohn, "Francis Farquhar at 84 Speaks of the Sierra Club—Then and Now," *Sierra Club Bulletin* 57, no. 6 (June 1972), 8–14.

49. Clyde, "Up the East Face of Mount Whitney," *Touring Topics* (1931).

50. I am indebted to Robin Ingraham, Jr., for his careful compilation of Clyde's first ascents, as well as his comprehensive ascent list: "Norman Clyde's List of First Ascents in the Sierra Nevada" and "Norman Clyde's Ascent List."

51. Norman Clyde, "Up Mount Thompson from the North for the First Time," in *Norman Clyde of the Sierra Nevada: Rambles Through the Range of Light* (1971), 86–89. Clyde eventually climbed Mt. Thompson fifty times. Steve Roper, *The Climber's Guide to the High Sierra* (1976), 15.

52. Norman Clyde, "13,500-14,000 Foot Peaks," in *Close Ups of the High Sierra* (1976), 17–26.

53. John Moynier, "Sierra Six-Pack: Moderate Alpine Climbs in California's Range of Light," *Rock and Ice* 73: 72.

54. Norman Clyde, "An Early Ascent of the East Face of Bear Creek Spire," in *Norman Clyde of the Sierra Nevada* (1971), 75–78.

55. Hervey R. Voge, ed., *A Climber's Guide to the High Sierra* (rev. ed. 1965), 94.

CHAPTER 5

1. From an ad appearing in the *Los Angeles Times,* May 1, 1929; "Lecture Course Arranged," *Los Angeles Times,* February 6, 1930, A9. I thank Harv Galic of Stanford University for leading me to these references. In addition to Clyde, the Trailfinders lecture series included authors Charles Francis Saunders, Winfield Scott, and Edmund C. Jaeger. See

also Ronald C. Woolsey, *Will Thrall and the San Gabriels: A Man to Match the Mountains* (San Diego: Sunbelt Publications, 2004).

2. The information for this chapter is liberally drawn from Norman Clyde, "Over the Crest of Southland Urban Mountains: The Chronicle of a Mountaineer's Jaunt Along the Summits of the Peaks that Encircle Metropolitan Southern California," *Touring Topics* (April 1932), 10–21, 45–48.

3. I drew heavily on the two articles reprinted in the volume *El Picacho Del Diablo: The Conquest of Lower California's Highest Peak, 1932 and 1937* by Norman Clyde, introduction and bibliography by John W. Robinson, photographs by Nathan Clark (Los Angeles: Dawson's Book Shop, 1975).

CHAPTER 6

1. Norman Clyde is quoted by Francis P. Farquhar in "Mountaineering Notes," *Sierra Club Bulletin* 12, no. 3 (1926), 307. I am grateful to Steve Roper for bringing this to my attention.

2. Typewritten manuscript from the Norman Asa Clyde Collection, courtesy of the Bancroft Library, University of California, Berkeley.

3. Phil Townsend Hanna, "Norman Clyde," *Touring Topics*, November 1927.

4. David R. Brower, *For Earth's Sake: The Life and Times of David Brower* (Salt Lake City: Peregrine Smith Books, 1990), 28.

5. David Brower, in the foreword to *A Climber's Guide to the High Sierra*, by Hervey R. Voge, ed. (rev. ed. 1965), viii.

6. Tom Miller, "First on the Most: An Interview with Norman Clyde," *Climbing* (May–June 1972), 3–6.

7. Brower wrote, "We developed an interest in the entire question of placing summit registers and safeguarding their contents." Brower, in the foreword to *A Climber's Guide to the High Sierra*, by Hervey R. Voge, ed. (rev. ed. 1965), viii.

8. David R. Brower, *For Earth's Sake* (1990), 36.

9. As quoted in Ed Ainsworth, "Along El Camino Real," *Los Angeles Times*, July 6, 1934, A8. Clyde mentions that Voge and Brower were from Berkeley, and gives his own residence as Owens Valley; he also states that the three men were all Sierra Club members.

10. Ibid., 37. The results of the pair's labors would reach fruition twenty years later with the publication of Voge's *A Climber's Guide to the High Sierra* (1954).

11. Due to the incomplete nature of the mountaineering record, the actual total may be closer to two hundred first ascents and new routes.

12. Norman Clyde, "The First Ascent of Mount Humphreys from the East," *Sierra Club Bulletin* Vol. 21, no. 1 (February 1936), 49–53.

13. Norman Clyde, "Wintering in the Sierra Nevada," typescript in the Norman Asa Clyde Collection, Bancroft Library, University of California, Berkeley.

14. Norman Clyde, "The First Ascent of Mount Humphreys from the East," *Sierra Club Bulletin* Vol. 21, no. 1 (February 1936), 49–53.

15. Norman Clyde, "Skill in and the Enjoyment of Skiing," typescript, n.d. Norman Asa Clyde Collection, Bancroft Library, University of California, Berkeley.

16. H. A. Grinnell, *Annie Montague Alexander* (Berkeley: Grinnell Naturalists Society, in conjunction with the Museum of Vertebrate Zoology, University of California, Berkeley, 1958), 19-20. I am grateful to John and Margie Evarts for sharing this source with me.

17. Norman Clyde, "Skiing and Climbing in the Headwaters of Bishop Creek," *Sierra Club Bulletin* 23, no. 2 (April 1938), 36–39.

18. Ibid.

19. Norman Clyde, "Bear Creek Spire and Around It," typescript, n.d. Norman Asa Clyde Collection, Bancroft Library, University of California, Berkeley.

20. Doug Robinson, *A Night on the Ground, A Day in the Open* (La Crescenta, CA: Mountain N' Air Books, 1996), 19.

21. Norman Clyde to Dorothy Cragen, February 27, 1964, courtesy of Jules and Shirley Eichorn.

22. Dorothy Leavitt Pepper, "High Trip High Jinks" (1976).

23. Olivia R. Johnson, "High Trip Reminiscences, 1904-1945," an interview conducted by Terry Kirker, in *Southern Sierrans II* (California State University, Fullerton, Oral History Program and the Sierra Club History Committee, 1976).

24. The peak was later immortalized in Jack Kerouac's account of his climb with poet Gary Snyder ("Japhy Ryder") in *The Dharma Bums* (1958).

25. Harold Kirker, personal communication.

26. According to Michael P. Cohen, David Brower did not recall Clyde ever saying such a thing. Cohen, *The History of the Sierra Club, 1892–1970* (1988), 106.

27. Richard M. Leonard, "Mountaineer, Lawyer, Environmentalist," Vol. 1, an interview conducted by Susan R. Schrepfer (Berkeley: the Bancroft Library Regional Oral History Office and the Sierra Club Oral History Series, 1975), 16–17; courtesy of the Regional Oral History Office, Bancroft Library, University of California, Berkeley.

28. Tom Miller, "First on the Most," *Climbing* (May-June 1972).

29. As quoted in Michael P. Cohen, *The History of the Sierra Club* (1988), 109.

30. L. Bruce Meyer, "High Trip Mountaineering—1941," *Sierra Club Bulletin* 27, no. 4 (August 1942), 125–127.

CHAPTER 7

1. Clyde's first rescue experience was in the summer of 1921, when he helped search for a man mortally injured in a fall in Yosemite. Francis C. Johnson, "Hurry! A Man Is Lost," *National Motorist* (November 1934), 4–6, 21–22.

2. Ibid.; Recollections of Jules Eichorn, typescript, n.d., courtesy of Jules and Shirley Eichorn.

3. Ibid.

4. "Boy Survives Cliff Tumble of 2000 Feet," *Los Angeles Times,* March 19, 1929, A5.

5. "Young Lamel's Body Found," *Los Angeles Times,* July 17, 1930, A1.

6. Recollections of Jules Eichorn; for a full account see Michael P. Ghiglieri and Charles R. "Butch" Farabee, Jr., *Off the Wall: Death in Yosemite* (Flagstaff, AZ: Puma Press, 2007), 275–276; *Mariposa Gazette*, February 25, 1932. I am indebted to Jim Snyder for bringing this material to my attention.

7. Norman Clyde, "In Quest of the Lost in the Sierra Nevada," typewritten and handwritten manuscript, n.d. Norman Asa Clyde Collection, Bancroft Library, University of California, Berkeley.

8. Harold Kirker, letter, July 29, 1993; a friend and contemporary of Starr's relayed this information to Kirker.

9. "Notes and Correspondence: The Search for Walter A. Starr, Jr.," *Sierra Club Bulletin* 19, no. 3 (June 1934), 81–85.

10. Glen Dawson's written account, as it appeared in "Notes and Correspondence: The Search for Walter A. Starr, Jr.," *Sierra Club Bulletin* 19, no. 3 (June 1934), 83.

11. Francis P. Farquhar, "Sierra Club Mountaineer and Editor," an interview conducted by Ann and Ray Lange, in *Sierra Club Reminiscences* (Sierra Club Oral History Project, 1974), 21.

12. Clyde's reason for continuing on with the search is from a September 1933 letter from Clyde to Francis Farquhar, and is cited in William Alsup, *Missing in the Minarets: The Search for Walter A. Starr, Jr.* (El Portal: The Yosemite Association, 2001), 91.

13. Norman Clyde's account, as it appears in "Notes and Correspondence: The Search for Walter A. Starr, Jr.," *Sierra Club Bulletin* 19, no. 3, 84.

14. Norman Clyde, "The Quest for Walter A. Starr, Jr.," in *Norman Clyde of the Sierra Nevada: Rambles Through the Range of Light* (1971), 71.

15. Tom Miller, "First on the Most: An Interview with Norman Clyde," *Climbing* (May-June 1972), 6.

16. Jules Eichorn, personal communication, October 16, 1993. William Alsup has thoroughly researched these events, and Steve Roper, following an examination of the gravesite in 1999, believes that much of this account can be called into question. William Alsup, *Missing in the Minarets: The Search for Walter A. Starr, Jr.* (2001).

17. From the Norman Asa Clyde Collection, Bancroft Library, University of California, Berkeley. The article that Kehrlein referred to is on page eight and is headlined "Starr Finder Mystery Man of the Mountains. Norman Clyde Recovered Three Others; He Lives in Wilds."

18. Jules Eichorn, personal communication, October 16, 1993.

19. William Alsup, *Missing in the Minarets: The Search for Walter A. Starr, Jr.* (2001), 115.

20. Ibid, 118.

21. E. S. Erwin to Norman Clyde, September 6, 1933, and September 26, 1933, in the Norman Asa Clyde Collection, Bancroft Library, University of California, Berkeley.

22. Norman Clyde to Mrs. Carmen Starr, September 24, 1933, in the Norman Asa Clyde Collection, Bancroft Library, University of California, Berkeley.

23. Norman Clyde, "Perseverance," n.d., in the Norman Asa Clyde Collection, Bancroft Library, University of California, Berkeley.

24. Ibid.

25. Jules Eichorn, personal communication, October 16, 1993.

26. W. A. Starr to Norman Clyde, December 16, 1933, in the Norman Asa Clyde Collection, Bancroft Library, University of California, Berkeley.

27. Steve Roper, *The Climber's Guide to the High Sierra* (San Franciso: Sierra Club Books, 1976), 106.

28. From a letter written by Francis Farquhar and quoted in Walter A. Starr, Jr., *Starr's Guide to the John Muir Trail and the High Sierra Region* (San Francisco: Sierra Club Books, 1964), viii.

29. "Pair Hunted in Mountains Found Killed," *San Francisco Chronicle,* August 16, 1934, 1. Hrvoje "Harv" Galic of Stanford University has compiled the most complete story of the Rettenbachers; I am grateful for his exhaustive research and support in this endeavor. For more information, see his website "Lonely Grave in the Sierra," www.stanford. edu/~galic/rettenbacher/about.html.

30. "Blizzard Tragedy Told by Frozen Survivor," *Los Angeles Times,* June 5, 1935, A1; see also Norman Clyde to Chester Versteeg, Letter Number 6 (May 15, 1935) in Dennis Kruska, *Twenty-Five Letters from Norman Clyde, 1923–1964* (1998), 26–27. Clyde went on to complain about the "Owens Valley 'lunkheads,' the dumbest of the dumb, scarcely one of whom would have lasted fifteen minutes in such a raging blizzard," who had criticized his actions on that fateful day. Clyde stated that he "might have a fight on hand but I will fight the whole valley rather than toler- ate such miserable stuff." Clyde recounts the event in "A Tragedy in the Sierra Nevada," in *Close Ups of the High Sierra,* by Wynne Benti, ed. (Bishop: Spotted Dog Press 1997), 157–167.

31. Norman Clyde to Chester Versteeg, Letter Number 6 (May 15, 1935) in Dennis Kruksa, *Twenty-Five Letters from Norman Clyde, 1923–1964* (1998).

32. According to longtime Independence resident Mary DeDecker, the plane contained top-secret documents; the military officials were on their way to the coast to discuss the attack on Pearl Harbor when the airship went down. Mary DeDecker, personal communication, July 5, 1993.

33. Norman Clyde, "The Quest for an Army Plane Lost in the Sierra Nevada," unpublished handwritten manuscript, n.d., in the Norman Asa Clyde Collection, Bancroft Library, University of California, Berkeley. It is interesting to note that, following his dismissal from the Sierra Club in the summer of 1941, Clyde was now identifying himself as a member of the American Alpine Club.

34. Norman Clyde to Commanding Officer, Army Air Base, March Field, California, August 8, 1942, courtesy of Jules and Shirley Eichorn.

35. Norman Clyde, "The Quest for an Army Plane Lost in the Sierra Nevada," unpublished handwritten manuscript, n.d., in the Norman Asa Clyde Collection, Bancroft Library, University of California, Berkeley.

36. Ibid.

37. "Commendation of Civilian," memo written by Colonel Davidson, August 22, 1942. Major William C. Evans wrote of Clyde that "his handling of the men and the instruction given by him to them both on the trail and in camp at night was excellent....His skill made it possible to get the bodies out without undue delay. It is the opinion of the undersigned that Dr. Clyde could well be hired by the Army to prepare men for just such emergency work so that future crashes could be tended in this sort of terrain by experienced men so as to achieve successful rescues with a minimum of personnel and expenditure." Major Evans to Commanding Officer, Army Air Base, March Field, California, August 10, 1942, courtesy of Jules and Shirley Eichorn.

38. Colonel Joseph H. Davidson to Norman Clyde, August 22, 1942, courtesy of Jules and Shirley Eichorn.

39. Mary DeDecker, personal communication, July 5, 1993.

40. Recollections of Jules Eichorn, typescript, n.d., courtesy of Jules and Shirley Eichorn.

41. Art Argiewicz was a graduate of Tamalpais High School in Marin County, California. He was killed while serving with the Tenth Mountain Division in Italy during World War II. Harold Klieforth, personal communication, September 16, 1995.

42. Andrew Hamilton, "California's Old Man of the Mountains," *Reader's Digest* (October 1963), 168C-J.

43. Norman Clyde to Jules Eichorn, December 20, 1950, courtesy of Jules and Shirley Eichorn. Christopher Smith Reynolds was the son of the president of Reynolds Tobacco Company. Harold Klieforth, personal

communication, September 16, 1995. See also "Lookout Reports Mt. Whitney Bodies," *Los Angeles Times*, August 13, 1950, 1.

44. Crispin Melton Wood, "A History of Mount Whitney," unpublished master's thesis, College of the Pacific, Stockton, California, June 1955, 107, courtesy of Jim Snyder, Yosemite National Park Research Library.

45. Roderick Nash, *Wilderness and the American Mind*, 3rd ed. (New Haven and London: Yale University Press, 1982), 316–341.

46. "There's No Obligation to Assist," unsigned editorial, *San Luis Obispo County Telegram-Tribune* (April 7, 1995), B-3; Jennifer Warren, "What If We Ignored the SOS? High-Risk Sports Have Sparked a Backlash Among Frustrated Rescue Teams. Park Service, Others Are Considering Charging Fees or Creating 'No-Rescue Zones,' in Which Athletes Would Be Left on Their Own," *Los Angeles Times* (November 30, 1993), A1.

CHAPTER 8

1. "Clyde, Norman Asa," in *Who Was Who in America with World Notables* Vol. V, 1969–1973 (Chicago: Marquis Who's Who, 1973), 138.

2. Joseph Grinnell, "A New Race of Screech Owl from California," *The Auk* XLV (April 1928).

3. Joseph Grinnell, Joseph S. Dixon, and Jean M. Linsdale, *Fur-Bearing Mammals of California: Their Natural History, Systematic Status, and Relations to Man* (Berkeley: University of California Press, 1937), 263.

4. Harold E. Crowe, "Sierra Club Physician, Baron, and President," interview conducted by Richard Searle, in *Sierra Club Reminiscences II* (Sierra Club History Committee, 1975), 4.

5. Norman Clyde, "Marten Trapping in the Sierras," *Fur-Fish-Game*, January 1938. I am indebted to Jim Snyder for bringing this article to my attention.

6. Norman Clyde, "Wild Animal Visitors to My Winter Cabin in the Sierra Nevada," typescript, n.d., in the Norman Asa Clyde Collection, Bancroft Library, University of California, Berkeley. This account also appears in Norman Clyde, "Friendly Birds, Animals Share Food of Winter Dweller in Sierra Cabin," *Fresno Bee*, December 20, 1965. I am grateful to Gene Rose for this article.

7. Norman Clyde, "Solo Afoot Across the Sierra Nevada in Autumn," in *Norman Clyde of the Sierra Nevada* (1971), 104; Norman Clyde, "Three

Weeks in Autumn on the Middle Fork of the Kings River: The Sierra Nevada," in *Norman Clyde of the Sierra Nevada* (1971), 110.

8. Norman Clyde, "Angling for Trout in the Gorges and Canyons of the Sierra Nevada," typescript, n.d., in the Norman Asa Clyde Collection, Bancroft Library, University of California, Berkeley.

9. Smoke Blanchard, *Walking Up and Down in the World: Memories of a Mountain Rambler* (San Francisco: Sierra Club Books, 1985), 141.

10. Norman Clyde, "From the Largest Trees in the World to the Top of the Highest Mountains in the United States," typescript, n.d., in the Norman Asa Clyde Collection, Bancroft Library, University of California, Berkeley.

11. Norman Clyde, "Building Trails in the Sequoia National Park, California," typescript, n.d., in the Norman Asa Clyde Collection, courtesy of the Bancroft Library, University of California, Berkeley.

12. W. R. Carpenter, U.S. Employees Compensation Commission, to Norman Clyde, Sequoia National Park, November 7, 1933, in the Norman Asa Clyde Collection, Bancroft Library, University of California, Berkeley.

13. Norman Clyde to U.S. Employees Compensation Commission, November 23, 1933, in the Norman Asa Clyde Collection, Bancroft Library, University of California, Berkeley.

14. Norman Clyde, "Into the Sierra Nevada and Up Mount Darwin with the U.S. Geological Survey," typescript, n.d., in the Norman Asa Clyde Collection, Bancroft Library, University of California, Berkeley. The packer may have been Ed Sargent, owner of Glacier Pack Train, Glacier Lodge. Louise A. Jackson gives a date of 1947 for the Geological Survey operation. Jackson, *The Mule Men: A History of Stock Packing in the Sierra Nevada* (Missoula, MT: Mountain Press Publishing Company, 2004), 106–107.

15. Ibid.

16. Mary DeDecker, personal communication, July 5, 1993.

17. Norman Clyde, "An Artist Goes Trout Fishing," unpublished manuscript, n.d., in the Norman Asa Clyde Collection, courtesy of the Bancroft Library, University of California, Berkeley.

18. As quoted in Jane Fisher, *An Exhibition of Paintings by Robert Clunie* (Ventura: Ventura County Historical Museum and Bishop: North Country Publishing, 1983). See also Richard Coons, *Robert Clunie: Plein-Air Painter of the Sierra* (Bishop, CA: Coons Gallery, 1998).

19. As quoted in William E. Smith, "Norman Clyde: Last of the Mountain Men," *Fortnight* (June-July 1957).

CHAPTER 9

1. H. L. Branthaver to Norman Clyde, n.d., in the Norman Asa Clyde Collection, Bancroft Library, University of California, Berkeley.

2. Steve Roper, "Norman Clyde," in *The High Sierra: Wilderness of Light,* by Claude Fiddler (San Francisco: Chronicle Books, 1995), 19.

3. Clara Clyde Tomkies to Norman Clyde, March 12, 1933, in the Norman Asa Clyde Collection, Bancroft Library, University of California, Berkeley.

4. William Hawley Davis to Norman Clyde, September 24, 1931; and Ted Waller to Norman Clyde, February 4, 1934, both in the Norman Asa Clyde Collection, Bancroft Library, University of California, Berkeley.

5. Walt Wheelock, letter, June 30, 1993, and personal communication, July 18, 1993.

6. Michael P. Cohen, *The History of the Sierra Club, 1892–1970* (1988), 102.

7. "Grizzled Mountaineer 'On Top of the World,'" *Los Angeles Times,* September 22, 1963, H7.

8. Norman Clyde to Dorothy Cragen, February 27, 1964, courtesy of Jules and Shirley Eichorn.

9. Norman Clyde to Dorothy Cragen, October 9, 1964, courtesy of Jules and Shirley Eichorn.

10. Norman Clyde to "Polly [Katherine G. Connable]," January 28, 1966, courtesy of Jules and Shirley Eichorn.

11. Gene Rose, letter, June 25, 1996, and email, January 23, 2007. I am indebted to Gene for his first-person accounts, for the gift of Clyde articles from the *Fresno Bee,* and his many years spent chronicling Sierra Nevada history.

12. Norman Clyde, *Norman Clyde of the Sierra Nevada: Rambles Through the Range of Light* (1971), 169–172.

13. Mary DeDecker, personal communication, July 5, 1993.

14. *Verg Heil* translates to "Mountain Greetings."

15. Maribel McKelvy, letter, May 9, 1997.

16. Ted Waller, letter, March 11, 1996.

17. Hervey H. Voge to Francis P. Farquhar, April 23, 1939. In the Francis P. Farquhar Collection, Bancroft Library, University of California, Berkeley.

18. The Board on Geographic Names waited until after Clyde's death in 1972 to make the naming official. Peter Browning, *Place Names of the Sierra Nevada, from Abbot to Zumwalt* (Berkeley: Wilderness Press, 1986), 159.

19. Winifred Thompson to Mrs. Duncan P. [Kathy] Jackson, September 30, 1950; Kathy Jackson to Charlotte Mauk, October 10, 1950; Charlotte Mauk to Miss Winifred Thompson, November 27, 1950; all in the Katherine Goddard Jones Papers, Special Collections, Robert E. Kennedy Library, California Polytechnic State University, San Luis Obispo. I am grateful to Nancy Loe for bringing these letters to my attention. The "battles" between Clyde and Kehrlein are unspecified.

20. Charlotte Mauk to Miss Winifred Thompson, November 27, 1950, in the Katherine Goddard Jones Papers, Special Collections, Robert E. Kennedy Library, California Polytechnic State University, San Luis Obispo.

21. Richard Searle, "Grassroots Sierra Club Leader," an interview conducted by Paul Clark, in *Southern Sierrans* (California State University, Fullerton, Oral History Program and the Sierra Club History Committee, 1976), 55.

22. John Shoupe, letter, January 16, 1996.

23. Smoke Blanchard, *Walking Up and Down in the World* (1985), 147.

24. This essay first appeared in *Harper's New Monthly Magazine* 55, no. 326 (July 1877); it was later reprinted in *The Mountains of California*, by John Muir, Garden City, NY: Anchor Books, 1894.

25. Michael P. Cohen, *History of the Sierra Club, 1892-1970* (1988), 107. Clyde wrote his own appreciation of snow banners in his article "Storms in the Sierra Nevada: Interesting Cloud Effects Unfold as Weather Changes," *Motorland* 48 (January 1941), 4, 12.

26. According to Ted Waller, Clyde had a "personality conflict" with some of the Sierra Club leadership that led to hard feelings; the incident on Matterhorn Peak in 1941 is perhaps the most dramatic of such encounters. Not all of the leadership conflicted with the lone mountaineer, however; David Brower said, "I knew Norman Clyde from 1933 until his death, and liked him." As quoted in Michael P. Cohen, *History of the*

Sierra Club, 1892–1970 (1988), 109; Ted Waller, personal communication, March 11, 1996.

27. As quoted in Michael P. Cohen, *History of the Sierra Club, 1892–1970* (1988), 101.

28. When asked by William E. Smith if he had ever been married, Clyde gave this brief reply. Smith, "Norman Clyde: Last of the Mountain Men," *Fortnight* (June-July 1957).

29. Dorothy Leavitt Pepper, "High Trip High Jinks," (1976), 27–28.

30. Mary DeDecker, personal communication, July 5, 1993.

31. Glen Dawson, letter, June 23, 1993. In a subsequent phone conversation (June 27, 1993) Mr. Dawson related that nothing ever came of Clyde's friendship with the two women. Perhaps there was an attraction when he was younger, but as he grew older he became a "fuddy-duddy" and his clothes and appearance generally deteriorated.

32. Dr. Cecelia Hurwich, letter, September 30, 1993; personal communication, February 1994.

33. Mary DeDecker, letter, July 5, 1993.

34. "Grizzled Mountaineer 'On Top of the World,'" *Los Angeles Times*, September 22, 1963, H7.

35. Smoke Blanchard, *Walking Up and Down in the World* (1985), 134.

CHAPTER 10

1. James D. Carson, letter, July 8, 1996.

2. Norman Clyde to Jules Eichorn, December 12, 1950, courtesy of Jules and Shirley Eichorn.

3. Norman Clyde to Jules Eichorn, February 2, 1961, courtesy of Jules and Shirley Eichorn.

4. His photograph collection is now at the Eastern California Museum, Independence, California.

5. Norman Clyde to Jules Eichorn, February 2, 1961, courtesy of Jules and Shirley Eichorn.

6. Robert H. Sydnor, personal communication, June 14, 2007. I am indebted to Jim Snyder for putting me in touch with Mr. Sydnor.

7. Walt Wheelock, "Norman Asa Clyde," *Southern Sierran*, February 1973.

8. Norman Clyde to Dr. James W. Rowe, Santa Barbara Cottage Hospital, April 25, 1969, courtesy of Vida Brown.

9. Vida Brown, personal communication, July 9, 1998.

10. M. C. Miles to Mrs. H. C. McKelvey, August 18, 1969. Miles wrote, "Our son who is a doctor at Cottage Hospital where he was operated on talked to the surgeon who operated. He told my son Norman should have had it done a long time before, but saw nothing to indicate he would have trouble. They want it watched, however. I shall keep as close watch on him as possible, and if anything flares up will let you know." Courtesy of Vida Brown.

11. Thomas H. Jukes, "In Memoriam: Norman Clyde, 1885–1972," *American Alpine Journal* 47 (1973), 540.

12. Robert H. Sydnor, personal communication, June 14, 2007.

13. "Norman Clyde, Famed Mountaineer, Author, Dies at Age Eighty-Seven," *Inyo Register*, Thursday, January 4, 1973; Certificate of Death for Norman Asa Clyde, State of California, Department of Health Services, dated December 29, 1972.

14. The account of Norman Clyde's scattering is in Smoke Blanchard, *Walking Up and Down in the World* (1985), 130–135.

15. Thomas H. Jukes, "In Memoriam, Norman Clyde, 1885–1972," *American Alpine Journal* 47 (1973), 540.

16. Mr. and Mrs. Tom Ross, letter to the editor, *Summit*, April 1973, 41.

17. *Summit*, November 1973. For more information on Sheridan Anderson, see Christopher Reynolds, "Trout Savant in a Big Black Cape," *Los Angeles Times*, April 20, 2004.

BIBLIOGRAPHY

Manuscript Collections

Norman Asa Clyde Collection, Bancroft Library, University of California, Berkeley
Norman A. Clyde Collection, Eastern California Museum, Independence, California
Francis P. Farquhar Collection, Bancroft Library, University of California, Berkeley
Kathleen Goddard Jones Papers, Special Collections, Kennedy Library, California Polytechnic State University, San Luis Obispo
Sierra Club Members Papers Collection, Bancroft Library, University of California, Berkeley
David R. Brower Collection
Aurelia Harwood Collection
Thomas F. Jukes Collection

Manuscript Materials from Private Collections

Clyde family papers, courtesy of Vida Brown and Maribel McKelvy
Norman Asa Clyde correspondence, courtesy of Jules and Shirley Eichorn
Recollections of Jules Eichorn, courtesy of Jules and Shirley Eichorn
Winifred May Bolster Clyde materials, courtesy of Walter R. Bolster
Lists of Norman Clyde's first ascents ("Norman Clyde's List of First Ascents in the Sierra Nevada" and "Norman Clyde's Ascent List," both by Robin Ingraham, Jr.), Sierra Club Registers, and History of Mountain Register materials, courtesy of Robin Ingraham, Jr.

Newspapers

Fresno Bee
Great Falls [Montana] Tribune
Inyo Independent
Inyo Register
Los Angeles Times
Mariposa (County) Gazette
San Francisco Chronicle
San Francisco Examiner
San Luis Obispo (Co.) Telegram–Tribune

Published Oral History Interviews

"Conversation between Omie Mairs and Mary Millman re: Halloween Incident and Norman Clyde, 1928." Tape recorded interview, Independence, California, July 1974, in the Norman A. Clyde Collection, Eastern California Museum, Independence, California.

Crowe, Harold E. "Sierra Club Physician, Baron, and President." Interview conducted by Richard Searle. *Sierra Club Reminiscences II*. Sierra Club Oral History Project, Sierra Club History Committee, 1975.

Dawson, Glen. "Pioneer Rock Climber and Ski Mountaineer." Interview conducted by Richard Searle. *Sierra Club Reminiscences II*. Sierra Club Oral History Project, Sierra Club History Committee, 1975.

Farquhar, Francis P. "Sierra Club Mountaineer and Editor." Interview conducted by Ann and Ray Lange. *Sierra Club Reminiscences*. Sierra Club Oral History Project, Sierra Club History Committee, 1974.

Johnson, Olivia R. "High Trip Reminiscences." *Southern Sierrans II*. Sierra Club Oral History Project, Sierra Club History Committee, 1977.

Leonard, Richard M. "Mountaineer, Lawyer, Environmentalist." Two volumes. Interview conducted by Susan R. Schrepfer. Courtesy of the Regional Oral History Office and the Sierra Club Oral History Series, Bancroft Library, University of California, Berkeley, 1975.

Mendenhall, John and Ruth. "Forty Years of Sierra Club Mountaineering Leadership, 1938–1978." *Southern Sierrans III*. Sierra Club Oral History Project, Sierra Club History Committee, 1980.

Pepper, Dorothy Leavitt. "High Trip High Jinks." Interview conducted by Terry Kirker. *Southern Sierrans*. Sierra Club Oral History Project; California State University, Fullerton, Oral History Program and the Sierra Club History Committee, 1976.

Searle, Richard. "Grassroots Sierra Club Leader." Interview conducted by Paul Clark. *Southern Sierrans*. Sierra Club Oral History Project; California State University, Fullerton, Oral History Program and the Sierra Club History Committee, 1976.

Conversations, Interviews, and Personal Correspondence with the Author

Roger Baer, letter, October 12, 1993
Richard Beach, personal communication, February 11, 1995
Barbara Norris Bedayn, personal communication, September 13, 1993
Dave Bohn, letter, May 16, 1997
Walter R. Bolster, letters, 1997
Beryl W. Brewer, letter, July 30, 1993
Vida Brown, letters and personal communication, 1997–1999
David M. Carson, letters, 1996–1998
James D. Carson, letter, July 8, 1996

Tyler Conrad (Sequoia Natural History Association Executive Director), personal communication, 1995

Jack Davis, letter, September 9, 1994

Glen Dawson, letter, June 23, 1993; personal communication, June 27, 1993

Mary DeDecker, letter, November 25, 1992; personal communication, July 5, 1993

Jules Eichorn, personal communication, October 16, 1993

John Evarts, personal communication, June 6, 2003

Alberta Wright Gerould, letter, April 12, 1995

John Harlin (editor of *Summit*), letter, July 1, 1995

Huston Horn, letter, September 22, 1994

Cecelia Hurwich, letter, September 30, 1993; personal communication, February 1994

Russell Huse, personal communication, April 8, 1995

Tom Kendall, letter, May 20, 1995

Jonathan F. King (editor of *Sierra*), letter, September 5, 1994

Harold Kirker, letters and personal communications, 1984 to 2007

Harold Klieforth, personal communication, September 16, 1995; letter, March 16, 1997

Russ Leadabrand, personal communication, 1992-1994

Norman B. Livermore, Jr., personal communication, April 1996

Jean Cleghorn McEuen, letter, October 4, 1993

Clara Clyde Tomkies McKeever, letters, 1997

Maribel McKelvy, letters and personal communication, 1997–1998

Norman Milleron, personal communication, September 10, 2002

Mary Millman, letters, May 1997

Jim Nichols, personal communication, March 16, 1995

Erika Perloff, personal communication, June 1, 2001

John W. Robinson, letter, August 26, 1993

Eugene Rose, personal communication, 1995 to 2007

Carl Sharsmith, letter, January 31, 1993

Lou Shober, personal communication, March 14, 1999

John Shoupe, letter, January 16, 1996

James Snyder, letters and personal communications, 1992 to 2007

William I. Stewart, letter, October 4, 1994

Robert H. Sydnor, personal communication, June 14, 2007

Robert Thornburg, letter, January 1, 1995

William Voss, letter, September 18, 1994

Ted Waller, letter, March 11, 1996

Walt Wheelock, letter, June 30, 1993; personal communication, July 18, 1993

Published Articles by Norman Clyde

"College Recreation." *The Geneva Cabinet*, n.d.

"May (A Reverie)." *The Geneva Cabinet*, n.d.

"The Mountain Brook." *The Geneva Cabinet* 30, no. 1 (October 1906).

"A Winter Sunrise." *The Geneva Cabinet* (February 1907).

"Roughing It on the Great Lakes." *The Geneva Cabinet* 33, no. 3 (December 1909).

"First Ascent of Mount Wilbur." *Sierra Club Bulletin* 12, no. 1 (1924).

"Ascent of Mount Merritt." *Sierra Club Bulletin* 12, no. 2 (1925).

"Mountaineering in the Rockies." *Sierra Club Bulletin* 12, no. 4 (1927).

"The First Ascent of Mount Russell." *Sierra Club Bulletin* 12, no. 4 (1927).

"A May Day Ascent of Mt. Whitney." *Touring Topics* (June 1927).

"Mountaineering in the Sierra Nevada." *Touring Topics* (July 1927).

"Scaling Mount Humphreys." *Touring Topics* (August 1927).

"The Ascent of Mount Darwin." *Touring Topics* (November 1927).

"Evolution Lake." *National Motorist* (January 1928).

"Climbing the Sierra Nevada from the Owens Valley." *Sierra Club Bulletin* 13, no. 1 (February 1928).

"The First Ascent of Mt. Mallory and Mt. Irvine." *Touring Topics* (March 1928).

"'Close Ups' of Our High Sierra." *Touring Topics* (April, May, June, July 1928).

"The Sierra Club Ascent of Mount Geikie." *Sierra Club Bulletin* 14, no. 1 (February 1929).

"Sierra Club Ascents in the Canadian Rockies." *American Alpine Journal* I (1929–1932): 7–15.

"The Beartooth Mountains of Montana." *American Alpine Journal* I (1929–1932): 174–181.

"Climbing the North Face of the North Palisade." *American Alpine Journal* I (1929–1932): 186–188.

"New Expeditions" (accounts of first ascents of routes on Middle Palisade and North Palisade). *American Alpine Journal* I (1929–1932): 395–401.

"A Mountaineer's Route to the Summit of Mt. Whitney," *American Alpine Journal* I (1929–1932): 415–417.

"High-Low: The Story of a Sunrise-to-Sunset Journey from the Summit of Mt. Whitney to Death Valley." *Touring Topics* (November 1930), 30–31.

"Difficult Peaks of the Sierra Nevada." *American Alpine Journal* 1, no. 3 (1931).

"Up the Middle Palisade." *Touring Topics* (August 1931).

"Mountains of the South Fork of the San Joaquin." *Southern California Banker* (November 1931).

"Up the East Face of Mount Whitney." *Touring Topics* (December 1931).

"Over the Crest of Southland Urban Mountains: The Chronicle of a Mountaineer's Jaunt Along the Summits of the Peaks that Encircle Metropolitan Southern California." *Touring Topics* (April 1932).

"Over the Sierra from Sequoia to Whitney." *Touring Topics* (July 1933).

"Scrambles on Bear Creek Spire, Sierra Nevada (First Ascent from the East)." *American Alpine Journal* II (1933–1936): 93–96.

"Death on a Mountaintop." *Westways* (May 1934).

"Glaciers of the Sierra Nevada." *Westways* (September 1935).
"The First Ascent of Mount Humphreys from the East." *Sierra Club Bulletin* 21, no. 1 (February 1936).
"Marten Trapping in the Sierras." *Fur-Fish-Game* (January 1938).
"Skiing and Climbing in the Headwaters of Bishop Creek." *Sierra Club Bulletin* 23, no. 2 (April 1938).
"Storms in the Sierra Nevada: Interesting Cloud Effects Unfold as Weather Changes." *Motorland* 48 (January 1941): 4, 12.
"Up Bear Creek Spire in a Summer Storm." *Westways* (July 1941).
"Climbs in the Palisades." *Sierra Club Bulletin* 35, no. 6 (June 1950): 127–129.
"Friendly Birds, Animals Share Food of Winter Dweller in Sierra Cabin." *Fresno Bee* (December 20, 1965).

Articles about Norman Clyde

Blevins, Winfred. "A Mountaineer's Vision." *Westways* (October 1974).
Falk, Burton. "Norman Clyde: Giant of the Sierra." *Summit* (May–June 1989).
Fertig, Fred. "Norman Clyde, Mountaineer." *Out West* (Fall 1967).
Gilliam, Harold. "Old Man of the Mountains." *San Francisco Sunday Chronicle*, August 13, 1961, "This World" section.
Hamilton, Andrew. "California's Old Man of the Mountains." *Reader's Digest* (October 1963).
Hanna, Phil Townsend. "Norman Clyde." *Touring Topics* (November 1927). In the Norman Asa Clyde Collection, Bancroft Library, University of California, Berkeley.
Ingraham, Robin. "Norman Clyde." *Climbing* (December 1988): 95–96.
Johnson, Francis C. "Hurry! A Man Is Lost." *National Motorist* (November 1934): 4–6, 21–22.
Jukes, Thomas H. "In Memoriam: Norman Clyde, 1885–1972." *American Alpine Journal* 47 (1973).
Miller, Tom. "First on the Most: An Interview with Norman Clyde." *Climbing* (May–June 1972).
"Old Man of the Sierra." *Time* (June 20, 1960).
"Norman Clyde Dead at Age 87." *Summit* (January–February 1973).
Smith, William E. "Norman Clyde: Last of the Mountain Men." *Fortnight* (June–July 1957).
Rowell, Galen. Review of *Norman Clyde of the Sierra Nevada*, in *American Alpine Journal* 18 (1972–1973): 220–221.
Wheelock, Walt. "Norman Asa Clyde." Obituary in *Southern Sierran* (February 1973).
Wilson Neill C. "A Prodigious Climber of Mountains." *National Motorist* (April 1928).

Books by Norman Clyde

Clyde, Norman. *Close Ups of the High Sierra*. Edited by Walt Wheelock. Glendale, CA: La Siesta Press, 1962. Reprint edition (with new material) edited and designed by Wynne Benti. Bishop, CA: Spotted Dog Press, 1997.

Clyde, Norman. *El Picacho Del Diablo: The Conquest of Lower California's Highest Peak, 1932 and 1937*. Introduction and bibliography by John W. Robinson. Photographs by Nathan Clark. Los Angeles: Dawson's Book Shop, 1975.

Clyde, Norman. *Norman Clyde of the Sierra Nevada: Rambles Through the Range of Light*. San Francisco: Scrimshaw Press, 1971.

Published Works

Alsup, William. *Missing in the Minarets: The Search for Walter A. Starr, Jr.* El Portal, CA: The Yosemite Association, 2001.

Blanchard, Smoke. *Walking Up and Down in the World: Memories of a Mountain Rambler*. San Francisco: Sierra Club Books, 1985.

Brower, David. *For Earth's Sake: The Life and Times of David Brower*. Salt Lake City: Peregrine Smith Books, 1990.

Browning, Peter. *Place Names of the Sierra Nevada, from Abbot to Zumwalt*. Berkeley: Wilderness Press, 1986.

Carson, David M. *Pro Christo et Patria: A History of Geneva College*. Virginia Beach, VA: The Donning Company, 1997.

Cohen, Michael P. *The History of the Sierra Club, 1892–1970*. San Francisco: Sierra Club Books, 1988.

Coons, Richard. *Robert Clunie: Plein-Air Painter of the Sierra*. Bishop, CA: Coons Gallery, 1998.

Croft, Peter, and Wynne Benti. *Climbing Mount Whitney*. Bishop, CA: Spotted Dog Press, 2005.

Dilsaver, Lary M., and William C. Tweed. *Challenge of the Big Trees: A Resource History of Sequoia and Kings Canyon National Parks*. Three Rivers, CA: Sequoia Natural History Association, 1990.

Eichorn, Arthur Francis, Sr. *The Mount Shasta Story*. Mt. Shasta: Mt. Shasta Herald, 1957.

Farquhar, Francis P. *History of the Sierra Nevada*. Berkeley and Los Angeles: University of California Press, 1965.

Fiddler, Claude. *The High Sierra: Wilderness of Light*. San Francisco: Chronicle Books, 1995.

Fisher, Jane. *An Exhibition of Paintings by Robert Clunie*. Museum Arts Committee of the Ventura County Historical Museum, Ventura, California, May 7 through May 29, 1983. Bishop, CA: North Country Publishing, 1983.

Ghiglieri, Michael P., and Charles R. "Butch" Farabee. *Off the Wall: Death in Yosemite*. Flagstaff: Puma Press, 2007.

Gilliam, Ann, ed. *Voices for the Earth: A Treasury of the* Sierra Club Bulletin, *1893–1977*. San Francisco: Sierra Club Books, 1979.

Grinnell, H. A. *Annie Montague Alexander*. Berkeley: Grinnell Naturalists Society, in conjunction with the Museum of Vertebrate Zoology, University of California, Berkeley, 1958.

Grinnell, Joseph, Joseph S. Dixon, and Jean M. Linsdale. *Fur-Bearing Mammals of California: Their Natural History, Systematic Status, and Relations to Man*. Berkeley and Los Angeles: University of California Press, 1937.

Jackson, Louise A. *The Mule Men: A History of Stock Packing in the Sierra Nevada*. Missoula, MT: Mountain Press Publishing Company, 2004.

Jones, Chris. *Climbing in North America*. Berkeley and Los Angeles: University of California Press, 1976.

Irwin, Sue. *California's Eastern Sierra: A Visitor's Guide*. Los Olivos, CA: Cachuma Press, 1991.

Kephart, Horace. *Camping and Woodcraft*. New York: Macmillan and Company, 1921.

Kimes, William F., and Maymie B. Kimes. *John Muir: A Reading Bibliography*. Fresno: Panorama West Books, 1986.

Kruska, Dennis. *Twenty-Five Letters from Norman Clyde, 1923–1964*. Los Angeles: Dawson's Book Shop, 1998.

Muir, John. *The Mountains of California*. Garden City, NY: Anchor Books, Doubleday and Company, Inc., 1961.

Nash, Roderick. *Wilderness and the American Mind*. 3rd Ed. New Haven and London: Yale University Press, 1982.

O'Neill, Elizabeth Stone. *Mountain Sage: The Life Story of Carl Sharsmith, Yosemite's Famous Ranger/Naturalist*. Yosemite National Park: Yosemite Association, 1988.

Peattie, Roderick, ed. *The Sierra Nevada: The Range of Light*. New York: The Vanguard Press, Inc., 1947.

Reid, Robert Leonard, ed. *A Treasury of the Sierra Nevada*. Berkeley: Wilderness Press, 1983.

Robbins, Royal. *Advanced Rockcraft*. Glendale, CA: La Siesta Press, 1973.

Robinson, Doug. *A Night on the Ground, A Day in the Open*. La Crescenta, CA: Mountain N' Air Books, 1996.

Roper, Steve. *The Climber's Guide to the High Sierra*. San Francisco: Sierra Club Books, 1976.

Roper, Steve, and Allen Steck. *Fifty Classic Climbs of North America*. San Francisco: Sierra Club Books, 1979.

Rose, Gene. *High Odyssey*. Fresno: Panorama West Books, 1987.

Snyder, Susan. *Past Tents: The Way We Camped*. Berkeley: Heyday Books, in collaboration with the Bancroft Library, University of California, Berkeley, 2006.

Starr, Walter A., Jr. *Starr's Guide to the John Muir Trail and the High Sierra Region*. San Francisco: Sierra Club Books, 1964.

Voge, Hervey H., ed. *A Climber's Guide to the High Sierra*. San Francisco: Sierra Club, 1954. Rev. ed., 1965.

Wampler, Joseph, and Weldon F. Heald. *High Sierra Mountain Wonderland*. Berkeley: Joseph Wampler, 1960.

Who's Who in America Vol. 34 (1966–1967). Chicago: Marquis Who's Who, Inc., 1967.

Who Was Who in America with World Notables Vol. 5 (1969–1973). Chicago: Marquis Who's Who, Inc., 1973.

Woolsey, Ronald C. *Will Thrall and the San Gabriels: A Man to Match the Mountains*. San Diego: Sunbelt Publications, 2004.

Published Articles

Ainsworth, Ed. "Along El Camino Real." *Los Angeles Times,* July 6, 1934.

"Blizzard Tragedy Told by Frozen Survivor." *Los Angeles Times,* June 5, 1935.

Bohn, Dave. "Francis Farquhar at 84 Speaks of the Sierra Club—Then and Now." *Sierra Club Bulletin* 57, no. 6 (June 1972).

"Boy Survives Cliff Tumble of 2000 Feet." *Los Angeles Times,* March 19, 1929.

Dawson, Ernest. "Climbing the Grand Teton. I. The First Sierra Club Party." *Sierra Club Bulletin* 12, no. 4 (1927).

Dawson, Glen. "Mountaineering Notes: Mountain Climbing on the 1931 Outing." *Sierra Club Bulletin* 17, no. 1 (February 1932).

Dawson, Michael. "My Father's Mount Whitney." *Westways* (April 1998): 72.

Farquhar, Francis P. "Mountaineering Notes." *Sierra Club Bulletin* 12, no. 3 (1926).

"Glacier Park Peak Scaled First Time. Four California Men, Sierra Club Members, Climb Mount Kinnerly." *Great Falls Tribune,* August 5, 1937.

Grinnell, Joseph. "A New Race of Screech Owl from California." *The Auk* XLV (April 1928).

"Grizzled Mountaineer 'On Top of the World.'" *Los Angeles Times,* September 22, 1963.

Huber, Walter L. "The Sierra Club in the Land of the Athabaska." *Sierra Club Bulletin* 14, no. 1 (February 1929).

"Lookout Reports Mt. Whitney Bodies." *Los Angeles Times,* August 13, 1950.

Meyer, L. Bruce. "High Trip Mountaineering—1941." *Sierra Club Bulletin* 27, no. 4 (August 1942).

Montgomery, Marion. "Ascent of Mount Robson—1928." *Sierra Club Bulletin* 14, no. 1 (February 1929).

Moyer, Wendell W. "The Beekeeper of McElvoy Canyon." *Newsletter for Friends of the Eastern California Museum* 10, no. 2 (Spring 1994).

Moynier, John. "Sierra Six-Pack: Moderate Alpine Climbs in California's Range of Light." *Rock and Ice* 73.

"Norman Clyde, Famed Mountaineer, Author, Dies at Age Eighty-Seven." *Inyo Register,* Thursday, January 4, 1973.

"Notes and Correspondence: The Search for Walter A. Starr, Jr." *Sierra Club Bulletin* 19, no. 3 (June 1934).

"Pair Hunted in Mountains Found Killed." *San Francisco Chronicle,* Thursday, August 16, 1934.

"Principal Resigned." *Inyo Register,* November 8, 1928.

Reynolds, Christopher. "Trout Savant in a Big Black Cape." *Los Angeles Times,* April 20, 2004.

Robinson, Bestor. "The Ascent of Mount Edith Cavell." *Sierra Club Bulletin* 14, no. 1 (February 1929).

Ross, Mr. and Mrs. Tom. Letter to the editor, *Summit,* April 1973, 41.

"*Summit* Presents the Award Winning 1974 Sheridan Anderson Abominable Mountaineering Calendar," *Summit,* November 1973.

"There's No Obligation to Assist." Unsigned editorial, *San Luis Obispo County Telegram-Tribune,* April 7, 1995.

Underhill, Robert L. M. "On the Use and Management of the Rope in Rock Work." *Sierra Club Bulletin* 16, no. 1 (February 1931).

"Want to Climb a Glacier? Southland Has One in Backyard." Photos by R. O. Ritchie. *Los Angeles Times,* August 24, 1948.

Warren, Jennifer. "What If We Ignored the SOS? High-Risk Sports Have Sparked a Backlash Among Frustrated Rescue Teams. Park Service, Others Are Considering Charging Fees or Creating 'No-Rescue Zones,' in Which Athletes Would Be Left on Their Own." *Los Angeles Times,* November 30, 1993.

Whittemore, Lowell. "Up Mount Whitehorn." *Sierra Club Bulletin* 14, no. 1 (February 1929).

Wilson, Neill C. "Climbing the Grand Teton. II. Some History and a Holiday Romp." *Sierra Club Bulletin* 12, no. 4 (1927).

"Young Lamel's Body Found." *Los Angeles Times,* July 17, 1930.

Unpublished Manuscripts

Engs, William D. "The Saga of the Registers." Typewritten manuscript, 11 pp., n.d. Courtesy of Robin Ingraham, Jr.

Leonard, Richard M., and the Sierra Club Committee on Mountain Records. "Mountain Records of the Sierra Nevada." Unpublished manuscript, 115 pp., May 1, 1937. Courtesy of Robin Ingraham, Jr.

Wood, Crispin Melton. "A History of Mount Whitney." Unpublished master's thesis, June 1955, College of the Pacific, Stockton, California.

Website

"Lonely Grave in the Sierra," maintained by Hrvoje "Harv" Galic, at http://www.stanford.edu/~galic/rettenbacher/clyde.html

Index

151

ACKNOWLEDGMENTS

D uring the course of researching and writing this book I have been the recipient of numerous kindnesses, from friends and strangers alike. My brother, Bruce, first introduced me to Norman Clyde's writings when we were fledgling climbers and explorers; he taught me the ropes. His critical reading of the text vastly improved the final product, and his guidance, support, and encouragement have been constant throughout my life. From our first meeting at U.C. Santa Barbara, Harold Kirker encouraged me to write the story of Clyde's life; as a renowned cultural historian, he showed me the route. Steve Medley, the Yosemite Association's late president, paved the way for this book's publication. Jim Snyder, another Sierra Nevada legend, offered not only encouragement and bibliographic support but helped bring this project to fruition following Steve's tragic death. I am grateful to the publications committees of the Yosemite Association and Heyday Books for seeing this project through to completion. Journalist and historian Gene Rose has been a part of the search for many years. Jules and Shirley Eichorn opened their home to me; it was an honor to interview this venerable climber. Norman Milleron was generous with the use of photographs from his private collection. Norman Clyde's family members—Vida Brown, Maribel McKelvy, and Clara McKeever—were open and forthcoming with information and insights into their uncle. Walter R. Bolster shared important photos and family history related to his aunt, Winifred May Bolster Clyde. Dr. Howard S. "Dick" Miller and Harold Klieforth both carefully read and commented extensively on the draft; their suggestions and recommendations greatly improved the final product. Dr. David Carson ferreted out several of Clyde's articles in the *Geneva Cabinet*. Robin

Ingraham, Jr., shared his information on Clyde's climbs, including first ascents, as well as his research into mountain registers. Harv Galic, of Stanford University, maintains a fascinating website, "Lonely Grave in the Sierra," that is an outstanding resource. George Thompson of the Center for American Places was an early advocate for this book. I have received the best treatment imaginable from Heyday Books, most notably my editors, Gayle Wattawa and Lisa K. Manwill, and the founder of Heyday, Malcolm Margolin. Several people listed in the notes and bibliography contributed letters, phone conversations, personal interviews, and photographs that helped me construct this biography; I am grateful for their time, energy, and reminiscences. The librarians and staff members of the following institutions kept me supplied with books, articles, and manuscript collections: the Eastern California Museum, Independence (Bill Michael, Beth Porter); the Bancroft Library, University of California, Berkeley (Susan Snyder); the Robert E. Kennedy Library, Cal Poly, San Luis Obispo (Nancy Loe); the Yosemite National Park Research Library, Yosemite (Linda Eade); the Sequoia National Park Museum, Three Rivers (Melany Ruesch); the Stanislaus National Forest (Pamela Conners); the Grand Teton National Park Museum (Christine Marie Jacobs Landrum); the American Alpine Club Library, Golden, Colorado (Lisa Webster); the Huntington Library, San Marino (Peter Blodgett); the Sierra Club (John Shoupe); and the Automobile Club of Southern California (Morgan Yates). Several important leads were the result of queries that appeared in *Yosemite* (the quarterly journal of the Yosemite Association), the *Los Angeles Times Book Review, Summit Magazine*, the *Newsletter for the Friends of the Eastern California Museum,* and the *Herald-Dispatch* (Huntington, West Virginia). Any loose hand- or footholds, false leads, sudden drop-offs, factual rockslides, or literary gaping bergshrunds are solely my responsibility.

My family and friends have heard about Norman Clyde for several years, and to all of them I am grateful for their continued interest and support. Lastly, I want to thank my wife, Rayena, for her love, encouragement, support, sense of humor, typing skills, companionship, and insights—little did she know that we would have an erudite, contentious, and fascinating houseguest for all these years.

ABOUT THE AUTHOR

Robert C. Pavlik is an environmental planner and historian with the California Department of Transportation. A native of Cleveland, Ohio, he was raised in the San Fernando Valley but grew up in the mountains of California, hiking, climbing, and traveling to remote places of quiet beauty throughout the state. He has worked for the California Department of Parks and Recreation, the Yosemite Institute, and the National Park Service. He is a graduate of California State University, Northridge, and the University of California, Santa Barbara, where he earned his M.A. degree in the Public Historical Studies Program. He lives in San Luis Obispo with his wife, Rayena.

YOSEMITE
ASSOCIATION

The Yosemite Association is a 501(c)(3) nonprofit membership organization; since 1923, it has initiated and supported a variety of interpretive, educational, research, scientific, and environmental programs in Yosemite National Park, in cooperation with the National Park Service. Revenue generated by its publishing program, park visitor center bookstores, Yosemite Outdoor Adventures, membership dues, and donations enables it to provide services and direct financial support that promote park stewardship and enrich the visitor experience. To learn more about the association's activities and other publications, or for information about mem-bership, please write to the Yosemite Association, P.O. Box 230, El Portal, CA, 95318, call (209) 379-2646, or visit www.yosemite.org.

**HEYDAY
BOOKS**

Heyday Books, founded in 1974, works to deepen people's understanding and appreciation of the cultural, artistic, historic, and natural resources of California and the American West. It operates under a 501(c)(3) nonprofit educational organization (Heyday Institute) and, in addition to publishing books, sponsors a wide range of programs, outreach, and events. For more information about this or about becoming a Friend of Heyday, please visit our website at www.heydaybooks.com.